# NO-NONSENSE KEY

Read *Understanding Condominiums and Co-ops*

- If you are interested in an easy, maintenance-free lifestyle.
- If you want to understand the differences between condos and co-ops and the advantages and disadvantages of each.
- If you want to find out if a condo or co-op is right for you.
- If you want to learn about vacation time sharing programs.

**NO-NONSENSE FINANCIAL GUIDES:**

*How to Finance Your Child's College Education*
*How to Use Credit and Credit Cards*
*Understanding Treasury Bills and Other U.S. Government Securities*
*Understanding Tax-Exempt Bonds*
*Understanding Money Market Funds*
*Understanding Mutual Funds*
*Understanding IRAs*
*Understanding Common Stocks*
*Understanding the Stock Market*
*Understanding Stock Options and Futures Markets*
*How to Choose a Discount Stockbroker*
*How to Make Personal Financial Planning Work for You*
*How to Plan and Invest for Your Retirement*
*The New Tax Law and What It Means to You*

**NO-NONSENSE REAL ESTATE GUIDES:**

*Understanding Condominiums and Co-ops*
*Understanding Buying and Selling a House*
*Understanding Mortgages*
*Refinancing Your Mortgage*

**NO-NONSENSE LEGAL GUIDES:**

*Understanding Estate Planning and Wills*
*How to Choose a Lawyer*

# UNDERSTANDING CONDOMINIUMS AND CO-OPS

Phyllis C. Kaufman
& Arnold Corrigan

**LONGMEADOW PRESS**

The authors want to thank real estate developer and lecturer Jack W. Blumenfeld, without whose advice, help, and wisdom this book would not have been possible.

Understanding Condominiums and Co-ops

Cover art copyright © 1985 by Longmeadow Press
Design by Adrian Taylor. Production services by William S. Konecky Associates, New York.

ISBN: 0-681-40241-5

Printed in the United States of America

0  9  8  7  6  5  4  3  2

To
Sandy and David Devins and Lois and George Bell,
dear friends who are always there when needed.

# TABLE OF CONTENTS

CHAPTER 1    Are Condos and Co-ops Right for You?    1
CHAPTER 2    To Rent or to Buy    3
CHAPTER 3    What Is a Condominium?    7
CHAPTER 4    What Is a Co-operative?    11
CHAPTER 5    Condominiums and Co-operatives: A Comparison    13
CHAPTER 6    The Benefits and Drawbacks of Shared Space    16
CHAPTER 7    How to Choose a Co-op or Condo    18
CHAPTER 8    The No-Nonsense Condo and Co-op Buyer's Check List    23
CHAPTER 9    Management    24
CHAPTER 10   Assessments and Maintenance Fees    25
CHAPTER 11   The Documents—An Introduction    28
CHAPTER 12   Rules and Regulations    30
CHAPTER 13   Condominium Documents    33
CHAPTER 14   Co-operative Documents    42
CHAPTER 15   The Interview    47
CHAPTER 16   Escrow and How to Handle It    49
CHAPTER 17   Calculating Your Down Payment    51
CHAPTER 18   Financing Co-operatives    53
CHAPTER 19   Financing Condominiums—Mortgages    54
CHAPTER 20   Settlement or Closing the Deal    61
CHAPTER 21   Time Sharing    63
Glossary    67
No-Nonsense Condo and Co-op Checklist    73
Appendices    81

# 1

# ARE CONDOS AND CO-OPS RIGHT FOR YOU?

Ownership of a condominium or co-operative is ideal for many people. The advantages of "shared space" living are attracting more and more Americans.

Compared with owning a home, ownership of a condo or co-op gives you virtually maintenance-free living, similar to what you might find in a well-run apartment building, but with the advantages of ownership. If you aren't the type to shovel snow, or if the thought of cutting the grass makes you sneeze, then consider the ease of owning a condo or co-op.

Or perhaps it's the shared recreational facilities that attract you. And if you are social, and like to get together with your neighbors in community discussion and activity, then a condo or co-op may be just right for you.

Compared with renting, a condo or co-op can give you the advantages of home ownership. And while ownership isn't necessarily for everyone, these advantages can be tremendous.

Condominiums and co-operatives are not a new lifestyle concept, though they came into prominence in the United States only about 20 years ago. Actually, communal living in cooperative, shared space environments dates back to before recorded history.

By the year 2005, fifty percent of the American people may live in some form of shared space environment. Condominiums now make up one-third of the total multi-family construction starts in the U.S.; this compares with only one-tenth a few years ago.

*Understanding Condominiums and Co-ops* will explain what's behind the condo/co-op boom. We will show you why so many young couples are buying condos and co-ops as "starter" homes, and why "shared space" living is rapidly becoming popular with retired people who enjoy the social, maintenance-free lifestyle.

# 2

# TO RENT OR TO BUY

The decision whether to rent or to buy is one that must be considered carefully and fully before you even begin to determine what type of property you want.

The first step is to prepare your own budget or "cash flow" statement. This will give you an idea of the amount you can spend each month for housing. Once you know what you can spend, you can determine what type of housing suits you best.

There are many different ways of setting up a household budget or cash flow statement. We like a simple 3-column setup, with one column for annual totals, and columns for weekly and monthly figures. The annual column must be filled in for each category; the weekly and monthly columns are to be used whenever convenient, both to let you see clearly how much you are spending and to arrive at the annual totals. A sample might look something like Table 1 (we're assuming that you're not presently a home owner).

It's an easy form to use. For some items, like auto insurance and vacations, you'll probably find it easiest simply to put in annual totals. For items that you usually think of in terms of weekly totals, such as food, put in the weekly figure and multiply by 52 to get the annual figure; for items that are usually paid monthly, such as rent, enter the monthly figure and multiply by 12.

Now, using a similar sheet if you wish, calculate your expected monthly and annual costs of owning a condo or co-op. Remember that as a home owner, you will have to spend not only for a mortgage or co-op loan (and probably for utilities, if they aren't included

3

|  | *Weekly* | *Monthly* | *Annual* |
|---|---|---|---|
| **Housing** | | | |
| Rent | $ | $ 400 | $ 4,800 |
| Elec. & Gas | | 80 | 960 |
| Total | | 480 | 5,760 |
| **Other** | | | |
| Food | 100 | | 5,200 |
| Household | 20 | | 1,040 |
| Meals Out | 35 | | 1,820 |
| Entertainment | 20 | | 1,040 |
| Clothing | | 100 | 1,200 |
| Vacations | | | 1,500 |
| Gasoline | | | |
| Auto insurance | | | |
| Life insurance | | | |
| Tuition | | | |
| Etc., etc... | | | |

in your monthly charges), but also for monthly maintenance fees, home insurance, and (in a condo) property taxes. (In a co-op, property taxes are included in your monthly fee.)

On the other hand, you will save on federal (and possibly on state) income taxes. Under the Tax Reform Act of 1986, you can still deduct the *interest* payments on your mortgage or co-op loan, as long as the home qualifies as your primary or secondary residence. Co-op owners can also deduct the portion of monthly fees that represents their payment of *interest* on the co-op corporation's mortgage. A condo owner deducts the property taxes, and a co-op owner deducts the share of property taxes included in the monthly fee.

Assume that the interest component of your payments is $800 per month, your property taxes amount to $400 per month, and you are in a 28% tax bracket. Your annual tax saving would be:

(12) × ($800 + $400) × (.28) = $4,032, or $336 per month.

Now, consider the *down payment* that you will have to make in buying a condo or co–op. Once you have done some shopping, you will know the price range in your area for the type of condo or co-op you want to buy, how much of the total price can be covered by a mortgage or co-op loan, and how much will remain that has to be covered by you in cash at the outset (the down payment).

To the down payment, you should add the amount of upfront cash you will have to spend for closing costs, attorney's fees, and your costs of relocating, including moving costs, new furniture, etc. If you don't have that amount of cash available, you will need to figure how much you can save per month and how long it will take you to build up the necessary sum.

Now take a hard look at all the above figures. Assuming that you can manage the down payment, can you also manage whatever increase in monthly costs is involved in becoming a home owner after taking the tax savings into account? If not, can you see ways to save on other expenses?

If you are now managing to save regularly every month, would you be willing to save less in cash, and to put part or all of your saving effort into paying off a mortgage or co-op loan and building up your owner-ship in your own home? A home may be as good an investment as you can find. But you may have to forgo the flexibility that comes from building up a cash reserve that you can get at quickly and easily.

Deciding whether to rent or buy is both a lifestyle decision and a financial decision.

Psychologically, ownership of your own house is a gratifying source of pride and security; and the financial advantages of owning a home are still very great. The tax advantages have been illustrated above. Moreover, we live in an inflationary world. If inflation continues, and it's hard to imagine otherwise, your home will usually appreciate in value. For many people, buying a home has been the best financial investment they have ever made.

However, if your job or other considerations should force you to move from your present location, ownership could present problems. Renting gives you freedom of movement. When you rent, you can easily pack up and move if you need to relocate. When you own, you put time and money into your property and you may be unhappy if you have to give it all up. Also, you will have to put your home up for sale and wait for a buyer before you can take your money out of the property.

Ownership can be a financial burden despite the long-run benefits. Each and every month you must be able to make a rather substantial payment to the mortgage lender, or else run the risk of losing your home. When you rent, if your finances become tight, you always have the option of moving to a less expensive location.

While renting means passing up the tax and ownership advantages we mentioned above, it does leave you more money to use elsewhere. When you rent, you don't have to tie up a substantial sum of money in a down payment, as you do when you buy. Instead, you can invest that money elsewhere and have it working for you and earning income for you every year.

The decision to buy may involve an element of guesswork when you are considering a condo or a co-op. When you own a house, there is more certainty about the amount you will have to pay each month. Decisions regarding repairs are largely up to you.

In a condo or co-operative, while the repayment of your loan or mortgage may be fixed, your monthly assessment, or maintenance fee, can and will go up each year, as the cost of everything rises. The decision as to how much you will have to pay for maintenance is not yours alone. It is determined by an elected board.

The decisions of the board go beyond mere maintenance. For example, the board can assess you a large sum to build a swimming pool for the condo or co-op. Even if you don't swim, you will be stuck with paying your part of the bill.

# 3

# WHAT IS A CONDOMINIUM?

## A Bit of History

Condominiums have existed for centuries. The word condominium comes from the Latin words "con", meaning *together with* or *in combination,* and "dominium", meaning *ownership* or *control.* So, condominium means ownership in combination with others, or joint ownership.

In 1961, the federal government passed legislation regarding condominium ownership in the U.S. Now, almost all states and some municipalities have also passed legislation covering condos and co-ops, and it is their legislation which prevails. Because regulation is up to each state and locality, condo laws can and do vary among states and even among municipalities within a state.

The U.S. condo boom began in the 1970s in California and Florida. Many condo high-rise developments were completed in Florida, only to find that the demand simply wasn't there. This seriously hurt the condo market nationwide, and is an important reason why appreciation in condo values has been at a lower rate than that of single-family homes.

## What Makes a Condo?

Condominium legislation permits individual living units to be carved out of a single larger property, with condo ownership consisting of two things—ownership of the individual unit and joint ownership of common areas. Condo laws allow many individual deeds to be

7

filed on record for individual portions of one large property, with each individual deed also sharing in a portion of a common deed for the part of the property that is not individually owned.

Any multiple-family structure or group of structures can be a condominium. This includes new and refurbished urban high-rise apartments, suburban townhouses, or single and multiple-family dwellings plus the grounds, elevators, lobbies and common space that surrounds the living units.

## What Do You Own?

In a condo you own your living unit. Or, to be more precise, in most areas you own the *air space* between the walls, floor, and ceiling of the unit in which you live. A condo is often referred to as an "air space estate."

You own the air space in "fee simple absolute" ("fee" for short). Fee is the same type of ownership that you would have in a single-family dwelling. It is the most complete kind of ownership one can acquire. It gives you freedom to use your space and to sell it or will it, without any restrictions of any kind whatsoever.

However, let us repeat that what you own in fee is the *air space* that makes up your apartment or townhouse. Unlike a single-family house, you don't own the exterior or communal walls, nor do you specifically own the land on which your own unit sits. But, because you have a fee ownership of the space, you can get a mortgage loan for the purchase of a condo, just as with a single-family house.

So you have complete control over the interior of your unit, but not over its perimeter. You can change an interior wall—for example, by drilling a pass-through between your kitchen and your dining room—but you would not be allowed to rip out the exterior wall near your front door in order to enlarge the door unless you got permission from the condo association. You don't own the exterior wall, you only own the interior space.

## Common Areas

Who owns the exterior wall? The exterior walls and other common areas (also called common space, common elements, common property, or common estate), such as the lobby, recreational areas, elevators, grounds, parking areas, grass and trees are owned in sum by *all* the owners of individual condo units.

Why? There are many reasons. One is that the external and communal walls, as well as the floors and ceilings, contain pipes and electrical wiring that service many units. If you owned the floors, for example, and your neighbor below had a leak in a pipe, you could theoretically make it very difficult for your neighbor to get his or her problem corrected.

So when you buy a condo, you actually own two things. First, as we said, you own the interior air space that makes up your particular unit. Second, you own an "undivided interest in the common areas." It is this undivided interest that gives you joint ownership, with all the other condo owners, of the common areas.

## Right to Use

Even though you are a joint owner, you are not an exclusive one. You don't have the absolute right to use the common areas, as you have with your own unit. The right that you own is a *joint* right, and the use of these jointly owned areas is determined by rules and regulations established by the condo board.

Do you actually own a piece of the lobby? There are two parts to the answer. The first is yes, you do own a piece. The second is, obviously, you don't own any particular piece. What you own is an *undivided interest in the whole*. Why? If you could go to the lobby and claim a certain piece as yours, it would be both silly and dangerous. Theoretically, you could then charge your neighbors a fee for crossing your part of the lobby to get to the elevators. This may sound ridiculous, but it is precisely why the law states that you own an undivided interest in all common areas, rather than a specific piece of one common area.

## How Is My Percentage Determined?

How is the extent of your undivided common interest determined? The most common way is by a mathematical formula in which all of the units in the condominium are totalled as to actual area. The pro rata interest you own in the common areas is proportioned according to your pro rata portion of this total. In some condos, extra points for the desirability of each particular unit are added in as another factor in the equation. But the more usual proportioning is pro rata.

For example, let's assume that there are 10 units in a condo, and each is exactly the same size. Each condo owner would then own a 10% undivided interest in the common areas.

Next assume that there are 15 units in the condo, 5 of equal size, and 10 others twice that size. Thus there are 25 (5 + (2 × 10)) ownership units. The owners of the 10 units would each own 2 × 1/25, or 8% of the common area, while the owners of the smaller 5 units would own 4% of the common area.


## Tax Ramifications

A condo which qualifies as your primary or secondary residence provides exactly the same tax breaks as a single-family house. You have a separate mortgage on your own unit, and the mortgage interest payments are deductible in calculating your federal income tax. Real estate taxes are also individually assessed and deductible. (See the No-Nonsense Financial Guide, *The New Tax Law and What it Means to You.*)

# 4

## WHAT IS A CO-OPERATIVE?

A co-operative is a type of corporation which is most popular in big cities such as New York. Each owner buys shares in the co-operative corporation. The corporation then gives each shareholder a "proprietary lease" (called a "certificate of beneficial interest" in some states), which enables him or her to live in the unit desired. Co-ops can be new or renovated high-rise buildings, garden-type apartments, or townhouses.

In a co-op, all the shareholders pay a pro rata portion of a common mortgage held by the corporation. The amount you pay individually is determined by the number of shares you own. You cannot get a mortgage to finance the purchase of a co-op unit, since you don't own the individual unit. What you get is a personal loan, and your shares of stock are used as collateral.

Since you don't actually own your unit, but only have a lease on it, you can take fewer liberties with it than with a condo. More individual items are regulated in a co-op than in a condo, because you don't have fee simple ownership of your living unit.

In a co-op, the number of shares you own is determined by the size, desirability of location and other features of the unit you occupy under your proprietary lease. Maintenance fees are determined by the elected board of directors and allocated according to how many shares you own.

### Common Areas

As in a condominium, you have the non-exclusive right to use common areas. In a co-op, common areas include all spaces in the complex not assigned to some-

11

one under a proprietary lease. The manner in which you can use these areas is specified in the corporate by-laws. (See Chapter 14.)

In some co-ops, portions of common space are specifically assigned to individual shareholders for their own personal use. This is especially true of parking and storage areas.

## Tax Ramifications

In some states, ownership of a co-op is not considered ownership of real property, but ownership of personal property. You should check with your attorney and/or accountant about the rules in your state. In general, however, the federal tax consequences of co-op ownership are the same as if you owned a single-family house or condominium. And, if the co-op is your primary or secondary residence, the interest you pay on your co-op loan is deductible for federal income tax purposes. (See the No-Nonsense Financial Guide, *The New Tax Law and What it Means to You*.)

# 5

# CONDOMINIUMS AND
# CO-OPERATIVES: A COMPARISON

We have already seen that the fundamental difference between condos and co-ops is the form of ownership. In a condo, you actually own your space in fee simple absolute, while in a co-op, you own shares in a co-operative corporation and hold a proprietary lease on your individual unit.

Because you have fee simple ownership of your condo unit, you have more freedom to do what you like with your interior space. In a co-op, you have to get the permission of the board for even the slightest interior alteration.

In a condo, the governing body is called the "homeowners' association," and it is in charge of operating the condo. The members of the homeowners' association are elected periodically and are in charge of determining the amount you pay as monthly dues (called "assessment") for the maintenance and upkeep of common areas.

In a co-op, the elected governing body is called the board of directors, and your monthly fee is called "maintenance." While the terms are different, the two work in almost the same way.

In both, the monthly fees cover the cost of upkeep and maintenance of common areas. The amount paid is only fixed for a short period of time when you first move in. After that, the board or association can change the assessment, or can assign a "special" assessment to cover the cost of new additions or extra or unexpected repairs.

In both forms of ownership, if the roof needs repair, it is the responsibility of the corporation or homeowners' association; but if the refrigerator breaks down in your own unit, it is up to you to get it fixed.

## Common Liability

Another difference is a by-product of the fact that you don't actually own your unit in a co-op. Because what you own is shares in a corporation, you are responsible for all corporate debts, in proportion to the number of shares you own as compared to the total number of shares. This is not true in a condo, where you own your own unit and have more independence from your neighbors.

Because of the potential for greater liability, banks and other lenders are often more reluctant to finance the purchase of a co-op. In addition, this potential for greater liability makes co-op boards very selective about who they allow to purchase shares in the co-op.

## Restrictions on Sale

In a condominium, you are free to sell your unit without restriction, to whomever you wish, unless the condo declaration and/or by-laws state otherwise. In a co-op, the person who buys your shares has to be approved by the co-op board of directors. It is the right of the board to refuse to sell shares to someone, as long as their refusal is not because of discrimination on account of race, religion, national origin, or sex, in some jurisdictions.

## Other Differences

Real estate taxes are assessed on each condo unit separately, while in a co-op they are assessed on the entire property. Co-op shareholders are given an accounting at the end of each year stating how much they have paid in taxes and mortgage interest. The amounts paid are deductible from federal (and sometimes state) income taxes.

Closing costs are considerably less in a co-op than in a condo. In a co-op, all charges relating to the mortgage and title to the property are paid by the co-op corporation. The shareholder usually pays only a transfer fee for the transfer of shares.

In a condo, all charges relating to the mortgage—including service and origination charges, title searches and insurance, and transfer taxes—are paid by the condo purchaser.

Any legal entity that can hold property can own a condo. This means that condos can be owned by a single person, by two or more people as joint tenants or tenants in common, or by married couples as tenants by the entireties. Corporations, partnerships, estates, trusts, etc., can all own condos.

Another rule that applies only to co-ops is called the 80/20 rule. This Internal Revenue Service rule states that at least 80% of the gross income of the co-operative corporation must come from monies paid in by the individual tenant shareholders, and not from rent or other income generated in the building (for example from commercial leases). If the 80/20 rule is violated, the co-op may lose its residential status, and you may lose your tax deductions for interest and taxes paid.

# 6

# THE BENEFITS AND
# DRAWBACKS OF SHARED SPACE

The main advantage of condo and co-op living is the easy, maintenance-free lifestyle. Many new developments include recreational amenities such as swimming pools, tennis courts, perhaps a golf course, or even horses and trails. The people who choose to live in these recreationally-oriented areas tend to have similar interests, and you can find a warm community spirit in the better-run developments.

Many people find condos and co-ops ideal for summer or vacation homes because of the amenities and the ease of maintenance.

Many retired people find the lifestyle ideal. Many young couples find the pricing attractive compared with the cost of buying a traditional single-family home.

With both condos and co-ops, your use of the common areas and, to a certain extent, of your own unit is governed by rules and regulations established by a board of elected persons.

Preliminary rules and regulations are established according to state law by the developer or co-op converter or sponsor, before the condo association or co-op board of directors first meets. These initial rules are filed with state and local governing bodies. Before you purchase, you will be given a copy of the rules, which become part of the many documents that are incorporated into the purchase agreement. You should be aware that these rules and regulations can and frequently are changed by the elected board, and not always to your liking.

When you live in your own house, especially if it is a single-family house that is separated from your neighbors by land on all four sides, you control your land and house completely. Unless you violate a law or ordinance, no one can stop you from doing just as you please with your land. Should you desire, you can plant trees, add a room, knock out interior walls, install new plumbing, or have five dogs and six cats. In short, you can do what you want, because you are the owner.

This is not true in shared living environments. The number of restrictions depends on the specific development, but you should be aware that limitations can be extensive and can cover such personal things as pets, children, interior usage and changes. Condos and co-ops are fine and convenient places to live—but as with everything in life, there are trade-offs.

# 7

# HOW TO CHOOSE A CO-OP OR CONDO

Location, location, location—This is the biggest factor to consider when you are contemplating the purchase of any property, including a co-op or condo.

We stress it particularly because many people pay less attention to location when buying a co-op or condo than they would if it were a single-family house. That's a mistake. Many co-ops and condos are downtown in large cities, and the location and the future of the city will affect your desire to live there permanently, your ability to resell, and the resale price. Remember that even though a co-op or a condo may look like an apartment, it's not. It's yours, for better or worse.

Of course, the same is true of a house. But it seems to be easier to predict the future of a suburban residential area, with such indexes of stability as schools, shopping, and churches, than of an urban area where your neighbors may be office buildings.

Of course, the convenience of being in town, near theatres and offices, appeals to many people, but you must consider the purchase of a co-op or condo as a long-term investment. Whether or not you will want to live there 20 or 25 years from now must enter into your decision to purchase.

You should also remember that most buildings appreciate (that is, go up) in value more rapidly when nearby buildings are used for the same purpose. So, if you are in a neighborhood surrounded by office towers, consider whether your unit will appreciate as fast as if you were in a more residential section.

One other important aspect of location is the size

of your unit and where it is situated within the complex. Actually, location is more important than size, and a smaller unit with a fabulous view, sunlight, and quiet will probably command a greater resale price than a larger unit on the ground floor with no view and street noise.

Comparison price shopping is a must. The only way to know whether your unit is a good buy is to check as many similar units that are on the market as you possibly can.

## Amenities

Next, look at the amenities offered. Remember that one of the joys of condo and co-op living is the maintenance-free environment. Check the condition of the common areas. Especially in an existing development, inspect the adequacy of maintenance. Is the decor of the public areas agreeable to you? Remember that the chosen decor in an existing property reflects the taste and style of the present owners, your co-owners. If their style annoys you or doesn't suit your taste, it might be better to look elsewhere.

## Financial Statements

The finances of the building are crucial to you, as a potential owner. Have your accountant look over the statements or projections. If you are considering an older condo or co-op, request statements for the previous 5 years.

## Construction—Older Building

Next, check the construction. You should treat the purchase of a condo or co-op exactly the same as if you were buying a house. If you are interested in an older building, be sure that the building is structurally sound before you invest. Remember that if something major goes wrong with the building, you, as one of the owners, must pay a pro rata share of the repairs.

How do you check a building for soundness? It is

best to be cautious and to hire a professional. In many parts of the country, inspection services are available which, for a fee of between $150 and $300, will check the building for structural soundness and for the condition of the heating, plumbing, roof, etc. Names of these companies are available by writing to the American Society of Home Inspectors, Suite 320, 655 15th Street, N. W., Washington, D.C. 20005. Always choose a firm with experience—one that has been in business at least 3 years is preferable.

If such services are not available in your area, we suggest that you hire the services of a structural engineer or architect. These professionals will probably charge you by the hour. You should determine the fees in advance. When you think of the expense of ownership, this fee is a small price to pay for peace of mind and avoidance of expensive surprises.

Have the engineer go over the entire building—not just the unit you want to purchase. You are of course interested in the soundness of your unit, but the health of the entire structure is vital as well.

## Construction—New Building

If you are interested in new construction, hire an architect to go over it with you. Remember that the construction is only as good as the builder, and his or her reputation is most important. Check other places that he or she has built. Talk with other people who live in the builder's housing—whether condo, single-family or high-rise apartments. Are they satisfied with the construction and with the services of the builder? Did the builder give good and courteous service? Were repairs accomplished promptly?

Be careful that all promises made in the promotional material or in the sample unit are fulfilled. It is a good idea to have your architect periodically check the development during the construction phase to make sure that all is well and that all building code requirements are satisfied. Usually, new construction is built under the Building Officials and Code Administrators International, Inc. regulations (known simply as the "BOCA" Code), or a local variation thereof. Your architect will be able to police the construction for code violations and can also make sure that the specific amenities listed in your agreement of sale have been incorporated into your unit.

You should also get an engineering report on the common elements, including heating, plumbing, electrical and mechanical from the builder. Compare this to the statement of your hired inspection service, engineer or architect.

## Soundproofing

If your unit is part of a multiple-family dwelling (a converted apartment house, for example), the need for soundproofing is nothing short of urgent. You want as much privacy from your neighbors as possible. If your neighbors play loud music, or if they rent to someone who does, you don't want to be invaded by their noise.

## Warranties

You should always check to see what warranties come with the building and with your unit. In an older building that is newly converted, the converter should provide various warranties against defects. Be cautious and inspect very carefully if you buy without any warranties. Living can get expensive as items in your home begin to fail.

In new construction, the builder may have purchased a 10-year warranty from the National Association of Homebuilders, called a HOW warranty (for Homeowners Warranty Corporation). A HOW warranty covers structural, but not cosmetic, defects and defects resulting from shoddy workmanship. It is by far the most widely used and respected warranty available today. Some builders issue their own warranties or have insurance companies insure the property against defect. And some states have made warranties mandatory.

All appliances should be covered by factory warranties. Read them carefully. Note whether the types of appliances used are the best or the poorest quality available in a given product line—this is a good clue to the overall quality of the construction. You might also want to upgrade your appliances, in which case a good builder should be glad to cooperate with you.

# 8

# THE NO-NONSENSE CONDO AND CO-OP BUYER'S CHECK LIST

Probably the most difficult part of home hunting is trying to remember what was in each place you saw on a given day. To help you eliminate this problem, we have included the "No-Nonsense Condo and Co-op Buyer's Check List" after the glossary.

We suggest that you photocopy the list and take it with you when you are condo or co-op shopping. Use one list for every unit you see that is a potential buy. The list is a great antidote for panic and confusion. If home shopping is driving you crazy, it may save your sanity.

# 9

## MANAGEMENT

Professional management of your co-op or condo will greatly enhance the quality of your life. There are management companies which specialize in the smooth and efficient management of condos and co-ops. Find out who manages the project you are interested in. Get a list of other properties managed by that company. Visit other developments to see how they are run. Ask questions of people who are familiar with the manager. Interview the manager yourself. Is the manager also a resident and available for emergencies at all hours? Understand the manager's philosophy, objective, and fees.

You should also investigate other companies that provide services—security guards, gardeners, engineers, and the like. Do your homework. Remember that in an older development, whom the board hires is an important indication of how they think.

If it is not a professional manager, but a group of residents who are managing the area, we suggest that you look very carefully before you buy. Most tenants are well meaning, but there is no substitute for cool, objective professionalism. See Chapter 12.

# 10

# ASSESSMENTS AND
# MAINTENANCE FEES

In a condo, the homeowners' association charges monthly expenses to the condo owners to cover the maintenance and upkeep of common areas and the salaries of employed personnel. This monthly fee is called your assessment or dues. The same type of fee is charged by the board of directors in a co-op. The co-op fee, called maintenance, is relatively higher than the condo assessment, because it includes a pro rata share of mortgage payments and real estate taxes.

## Budget

The first thing to determine is just what the monthly fee covers. A budget will be made available to you either from the condo association, the condo or co-op converter, the board of directors or the builder. Read it and discuss it with your attorney or accountant. Make sure that the charges are reasonable, and be wary if they are either too high or too low. An advantage of buying into an older operation is that it will have a monetary track record that you can see and rely on.

It is a good idea to check several developments or buildings in your area to compare costs of specific items and to make sure that the unit you are interested in is reasonable and sound.

## Low Balling

In a new development or conversion, you must watch out for "low balling." This is a device where the builder or converter absorbs many costs at the beginning so as not to reflect them in the budget. But once a certain number of units have been sold, the builder quietly steps away, and the condo association or board must then assume these previously hidden costs. In other words, the builder or converter subsidizes the operation for a given period, after which you find that you have more expenses than you bargained for.

## Reserve Fund

Part of your monthly assessment goes toward a reserve fund. It is called a reserve fund because it is a sum of money held in reserve for emergencies, such as the breakdown of the heating system or the sudden demise of the roof.

All co-ops and condos operate with a reserve fund. In new constructions or conversions, the builder or converter is supposed to fund the reserve to get it started. It is continually funded by a portion of the monthly fee. Most experts agree that the reserve fund should be no less than 20% of the total annual fees paid. Check the amount of the reserve fund, and if it is too low, think of buying elsewhere.

## Special Assessments

How else are emergencies handled? The board might vote a "special assessment," which can be charged in one of two ways. The first is a one-time lump-sum payment by every owner (often, though, this lump sum can be paid off in installments). Or, a smaller amount can be added to the monthly charge for a longer period of time until the repair or improvement is paid for. We favor the first way, even though it can mean a temporary burden, because once the emergency is paid for, your monthly fee returns to normal. When an added fee is spread over two years, let's say, it's more likely to become permanent, even after the emergency is paid for.

Let's say that your condo association has decided to build five tennis courts on the grounds. Unfortunately, you don't play tennis, and you wanted to build a swimming pool, but you were outvoted by the tennis buffs in the association. Now, let's assume that the cost of these five courts will be $100,000, and that the association has decided to pay off the cost of the courts in 2 years. If there are 100 owners, and you have one vote out of 100, this means that you are responsible to pay $500 per year for 2 years in added assessments. Ah, well—even though you don't play tennis, the addition of the courts will probably add to the resale value of your unit.

# 11

## Documents—An Introduction

When you deal with important legal documents such as those you must sign when you purchase a co-op or condo, it is important to seek professional advice.

All documents relating to condominiums and co-operatives must be filed according to law with appropriate state and local agencies. The condo or co-op cannot actually come into existence until the documents have been filed and approved. The fact that they are so filed is an important safeguard for purchasers, but knowing that they are filed is not enough.

Hire a lawyer, and choose one who has had experience in real estate, and especially with co-ops and condos. The first thing you should do is to ask friends or associates to recommend a good real estate lawyer. If you cannot get a recommendation from someone you trust, contact the local bar association. They will probably have a list of specializing attorneys for you to contact.

Make an appointment and interview the attorney. Ask as many questions as you think relevant. It's a good idea to make a list before your appointment, so that you don't forget important questions. Be sure to ask about the lawyer's fees and his or her experience in the co-op or condo field. Make sure you know who will actually handle your case. If you go to a large firm, find out if the lawyer you are interviewing will do your work, or if you will be relegated to a younger, more inexperienced associate. Make sure that you are completely comfortable with the attorney you select. If necessary, speak to several before deciding.

There are many documents to be understood and

signed when purchasing a condo or a co-op. We will first discuss the rules and regulations which follow the same general pattern for both condos and co-ops. Then we will treat the remainder of the condo and co-op documents in two separate chapters. We suggest that you read both chapters, even if one seems not to apply to you. It will give you a better idea of how these two legal entities differ.

# 12

## RULES AND REGULATIONS

In most discussions of the legal documents involved in becoming a condo or co-op owner, the rules and regulations of the condo or co-op are put rather low on the list. But none so directly affect your lifestyle and your freedom to alter, use, buy and sell your unit. If the rules and regulations are not to your liking, the other documents are irrelevant, since it hardly makes sense for you to buy that particular condo or co-op.

You will be given a copy of the rules before you buy. In both condos and co-ops, the rules are contained in the by-laws. Additional rules (sometimes called "house rules") often exist. Be sure to get copies of both documents. The house rules may be more specific, and you will want to be sure that you can live with them.

Read the rules thoroughly. They govern the way you will live. Don't buy into any building with the hope of changing one or more of the rules after you move in. Remember that the other owners have bought their units based on the existing rules and probably have no desire to change them. If something in the rules displeases you enough so that you can't live with it—buy elsewhere.

### What Do the Rules Cover?

How far can the rules go? The answer is very far, especially in a co-op. In a condo, where you own your unit, you have more autonomy. Rules can state how many people may occupy a particular unit, whether children or pets are allowed, whether or not you can rent (or, in a co-op, sublet) your unit to others, what hours you can use the swimming pool, where you can park your car, how loud you can play your stereo, and just about anything else you might imagine.

It sounds worse then it actually is, and you must remember that the rules are for your protection, too. Just as you can't make arbitrary alterations that might please you but damage the building or reduce the appeal of the unit to others, so the regulations requiring board approval will protect your investment when one of your co-owners wants to do something outrageous with his or her unit.

It is much easier to evaluate the rules and regulations and the way the board enforces them in an older property which has been operating for some time. In a new conversion or development, try to find out whether the developer or converter has a reputation for establishing good procedures and guidelines.

## Co-op Rules vs. Condo Rules

The rules and regulations tend to be more pervasive in a co-op than in a condo because, as we have stressed, you don't actually own your co-op unit as you do a condo. In a co-op, the rules often govern interior alterations that you want to make to your unit. Approval by the board of directors may be required for seemingly small internal changes. In a co-op, you should think of the space you occupy as if it were a rental unit. In a rental unit, would you be allowed to make the desired alteration without specific permission? If the answer is no, then the board of directors of the co-op will no doubt have to approve.

## Changing the Rules

Remember that the rules and regulations can be changed in accordance with procedures set forth in the by-laws. This may mean a vote of the board, or a vote of all owners by either a simple or two-thirds majority. Other variations are possible.

## Allocation of Fees

The by-laws also cover the allocation of monthly costs. Usually, as we pointed out earlier, these are apportioned pro rata according to the ratio of the space of your individual unit (in a condo) or the number of shares you own (in a co-op) to the total overall space or to the total number of shares in the co-op.

# 13

## CONDOMINIUM DOCUMENTS

There are many important documents to analyze and understand before you buy a condo. We will review them briefly. But we again stress the importance of consulting an attorney who specializes in real estate and has extensive experience with condominiums.

### The Declaration

The "declaration" (also called the "master deed" *or* "declaration of conditions, covenants and restrictions" *or* "plan of condominium ownership" *or* the "enabling declaration") is the legal document which fully describes all aspects of the entire condo area. It includes a map which shows how the larger area is divided into individual condo units, or air space estates, and it describes exactly what these estates consist of. For example, a particular declaration may state that a condo owner actually purchases the air space between walls and an·undivided interest in common areas, or from paint to paint within a given unit. The document will include either architect's renderings or, in some states, legal descriptions (without drawings) of the precise location of all buildings and other amenities such as swimming pools, tennis courts, stables, etc., on the property.

The declaration is the legal document which creates the condominium. It describes the plan of ownership and vests power over the condo in the board of directors, or managers. It is in this document that you will find your percentage of undivided common area and the percentage you must pay of the total amount of monthly costs. Have your lawyer check these numbers carefully. Remember that your percentage determines how many votes you have in condo affairs, and remember also that once the declaration is signed, it usually takes a unanimous vote of all the condo owners to change it. (Unlike a change in the by-laws, which usually requires either a simple or two-thirds majority.)

It is important also to know how your percentage of undivided interest in the common areas was arrived at. There are several possible formulas. Some states specify which formula must be used, while others are less rigid and allow other factors to enter into the calculation. In any case, the formula used will be described in the declaration. The most common methods of determining percentages are:

(1) In equal shares, so that each unit has equal voting power. This method of determination is most common in condos where all the units are identical.
(2) By taking the dollar value of your unit as a percentage of the total value of all the units in the condo. This percentage is then applied to determine your number of votes as compared with the total number of outstanding votes. This method is usually called the "fair market value" determination.
(3) The other common method of determining voting percentage is by taking the total living space of your unit as a percentage of the total living space of all the units combined, and applying this percentage to determine your number of votes.

**Voting Power Costs Money**

The more votes you have, the more power you will have to effect any changes and plans you desire. However, remember also that the more votes you have, the more monthly costs you will be required to pay, and the greater your percentage will be in case of special assessments.

34

## Limited Common Areas

Some areas in the condo development may be designated as limited common areas. These include balconies, patios, and parking spaces. In some condos, these areas are individually owned as part of the condo, but it is not uncommon for them to be jointly owned as common areas, with the proviso that the use of each area is restricted to the unit owner to which it is assigned.

## Recreational or Ground Leases

Before there was strict state and local scrutiny of condos, recreational or ground leases were a frequent problem. Under this practice, the condo builder or converter retained title to the recreational or parking areas which should naturally have been part of the common area of the condo. The builder or converter would then lease these areas back to the condo association, often for an excessive fee. Of course, these fees were passed on to all the condo owners.

Since the availability of recreational or other convenience areas influences the decision to buy, this practice has come to be regarded as deceptive. Many states have passed legislation against such leases. It is a good idea for you and your attorney to check the declaration and make sure that ownership of the entire parcel of land vests in the condo association, once the building or conversion is done. You don't want extra hidden expenses.

## Commercial Use

Some declarations provide for commercial property on the condo premises. If commercial establishments can rent units, are there any limitations on the types of businesses that can rent? Who gets the rental income? If businesses can buy units, do they have the same rights and obligations as the other condo owners? Do they pay an equal or greater percentage of costs (presumably they will use more electricity, parking and other essentials)? And finally, if they are assessed a greater percentage of the costs because of this greater use, do they have voting rights equal to or greater than those of the residential owners?

## HUD

If the condominium you are interested in is financed by a loan from the U.S. Department of Housing and Urban Development (HUD), the declaration and its contents will be strictly scrutinized by the agency to ensure compliance with its policies and programs. Among these is the assurance of meeting certain standards in construction and nondiscriminatory policies regarding purchasers. HUD also has a requirement that its "minimum property standards" be met by condo developers, and a HUD loan assures the purchaser of compliance with these standards.

## By-laws

The by-laws establish the condo government. All owners agree to abide by the rules and regulations established by the by-laws. (See Chapter 12.)

The by-laws state how the members of the board of directors of the condo (or homeowners') association will be elected, for how long they will serve, if they are to be paid, their powers, and the rules for removing board members. Rules for association meetings and special meetings are included. The by-laws state how many votes are required to pass a proposal, and how the by-laws themselves can be amended. Amending by-laws is usually by majority vote, not by unanimous vote as in the case of amending the declaration. The by-laws also include rules regarding when monthly dues or assessments are collected and the penalties for failure to pay.

## Right-of-First-Refusal Clause

Warning! Right-of-first-refusal clauses are an important matter, of great economic concern to you. Such clauses are more common in co-op by-laws than in condos, but they do exist in some condo documents, and you should be wary of purchasing any condo where there is such a clause.

A right-of-first-refusal clause requires you to offer the condo association the first right to buy your unit, should you decide to sell. This obviously hampers your free use of the property, and whether or not you are thinking now of future sale at an appreciated value, such a clause is not a good idea. It's worth noting that with FHA or HUD financing, such clauses are not permitted.

## Interviews

Even without a right-of-first-refusal clause, some condos require that potential buyers pass scrutiny by the board or a committee of the board. This restriction on your free right to resell might make you unhappy—or, on the other hand, you may appreciate some controls on your future neighbors.

## Restrictions

You must check the by-laws and declaration for any restrictions on the free use of your unit. For example, many condos do not allow pets or children. This may be perfectly agreeable to you, but you should certainly be aware of the restrictions. In addition, there may be limits on the number of persons occupying a unit, or on your ability to rent the unit to others and earn income from it. You should find out whether the condo is entirely residential or whether businesses will be able to locate in your home.

## New Condo Associations

Another problem worth mentioning is that of fledgling associations in just-converted or newly built condos. It generally takes a year or two before a condo association gets enough experience to begin running smoothly. Quite often, when the builder or converter turns the condo over to the association, a period of chaos ensues, marked by frequent violations of the by-laws and failure by some owners to pay their monthly assessment. It seems to be human nature for some individuals to take advantage of the inexperience of the new directors. So, if you have decided on a new condo or conversion, be prepared for things to be a bit chaotic for a while. In most cases, they will straighten themselves out in time.

## The Management Contract

The management contract is an essential part of the by-laws. Without proper management, condo life can be miserable.

A common trick is for the builder or converter to build in a long-term management contract for his or her firm. Long-term contracts can prove disastrous. With them, the condo owners have no effective hold over the manager and no way of ensuring good performance. A long-term contract eliminates the fear of being fired, and the management can easily grow "fat and lazy," knowing that they can't be dismissed before the contract expires without great expense on the part of the owners.

The problem of a long-term contract is even greater if the contract is with the builder or converter or one of their related companies. There is then a conflict of interest that works to the disadvantage of the condo owners, since the builder or converter has an interest in hiding defects and other problems until it is too late easily to remedy them.

Of course, no matter who the manager is, you should try to check his or her reliability, reputation and past performance.

## Management Contract Termination

Management contracts should include a termination clause, allowing the contract to be terminated "without cause." This means that if the condo board wants to terminate the contract, it does not have to prove that management misbehaved or did not perform properly. This keeps the management on their toes, since they know that they can be fired at any time upon short notice, usually no longer than 30 or 60 days.

## Condominium Sales Contract

This is the agreement of sale for your unit. It should fully describe your unit, and the number of votes it carries. Make sure that this number agrees with the number allocated to your unit in the declaration.

The sales contract (also called the "subscription and purchase agreement" or the "conditional sales contract") contains a complete description of your unit, with all amenities, such as appliances, etc., spelled out in full. It also states the sale price, the amount of down payment, the escrow agent(s), and the date of settlement.

Make sure that all the items you have negotiated appear in the sales contract. There is no guarantee of satisfaction on any item which is not included in this document. If the seller has told you that the carpeting is included with the unit, as well as all the appliances and the dining room chandelier, each of these items must be specified in the agreement.

If the condo is a new construction and you or your architect have made modifications to your unit, the details of these modifications must be written into the contract of sale. We suggest that you also include the right to inspection visits by you and/or your architect.

A copy of the condo budget should be attached to your sales contract, and it should also refer to the other legal documents, notably the declaration and the by-laws. However, you should never substitute the abbreviated version of these documents which appears in the sales contract for a thorough reading of the actual declaration and by-laws.

## Time Is of the Essence Clause

Very often, a "time is of the essence" clause will be in the contract of sale. This clause means that the buyer has only a specified amount of time—usually 60 or 90 days—to get financing, and if financing is not obtained within that time, the contract becomes void and all money is returned to the buyer. Actually, this is a good clause for both parties. It forces the lending institutions, who receive a copy of the contract with the mortgage application, to respond promptly.

## Insurance

The by-laws should make provision for fire, hazard and general liability insurance. Ask for copies of the insurance documents and make sure that all areas, including the common areas, are insured against fire, theft, and other hazards.

It is also important for the association to have public liability insurance in a substantial amount—at least several millions of dollars. This is needed to prevent economic disaster for the owners, should someone, for example, slip and fall in a common area while visiting an owner.

Of course, each owner should additionally insure his or her unit and its contents against fire, theft and other hazards. This insurance, usually known as homeowners insurance, should be obtained on your unit as soon as you sign the contract of sale. Upon that signing, you become what is known in the law as the beneficial owner. This means that while you are not yet the real owner, you are the future owner and you benefit from the continued security and safety of the condominium. The rule of beneficial ownership means that if the property is damaged by fire or flood or otherwise during the time between the signing of the contract of sale and the closing, you will still be required to close on the condo, and will have to pay the stated full price.

## Individual Unit Deeds

The individual unit deed is the specific description of your unit, as contained within the total condo property. It will repeat many of the words found in the declaration. The deed is the piece of paper that allows you the full right over your condo unit, subject to any restrictions in the declaration and by-laws, and gives you the right to sell and use the unit. As with a deed to a single-family house, this deed is registered (or filed) with the local government.

## Operating Budget

It is important for you to see a copy of the condo's current operating budget. If the condo is an older one, you should also ask for copies of prior years' budgets for comparison, and to see how assessments have changed over time. With a new condo, you should check the reasonableness of the amounts listed and, remembering low balling (Chapter 10), you should make sure that all necessary items are included. The budget ought to include the sum currently in the reserve fund and how much is added to it each year.

In an older condo, you should also request copies of the financial statements for the past few years. These provide a basis for analyzing how efficiently the property has been managed. In a new condo, of course, any statements are only projections, but you should check their reasonableness with the aid of your attorney or accountant.

# 14

## CO-OPERATIVE DOCUMENTS

Legally, as we have already seen, there is a great difference between a co-operative and a condominium.

### Certificate of Incorporation

The first and most important difference is that a co-operative is a corporation formed under the laws of a specific state. There must be a document, filed with the state, establishing the existence of the corporation. This is called the "certificate of incorporation" or, in some states, the "corporate charter."

The contents of the certificate of incorporation are usually standard and not very informative. The certificate states the purpose of the corporation, its name and address, and its life span—which is usually perpetual, or existing forever.

The certificate does not contain a description of each unit, nor does it contain architect's drawings as does the declaration of a condominium. Remember that co-op owners do not own individual units—the co-op corporation owns everything, and the individual owners merely own shares in the whole.

The certificate also states the total number of shares in the corporation and their par value. The par value is usually stated as a minimal amount, often $1.00 per share. Don't worry about it. Par value is a legal term that has nothing to do with the actual value of the stock.

Title to the property is held by the co-op corporation and passes to the corporation by deed. The deed is filed with the appropriate local authority.

## Corporate By-laws

The co-op by-laws are similar to the condo by-laws described in Chapter 13. The by-laws establish the rules and regulations for running the corporation.

As in a condo, the by-laws establish the rules for electing directors, their length of term, their compensation, if any, and their removal from office. Removal of directors is important, since stockholders usually do not have the right to veto the actions of directors, and usually the only way to stop the directors from taking unpopular actions is to remove them from office.

The by-laws will also state whether or not you can sublet your unit and, if so, for how long. The amount of cash that you must put down on buying into the co-op will be covered. Some co-ops in New York City require that you pay for your shares in cash, without financing, while others will accept those who can afford to pay 50% in cash.

## Right-of-First-Refusal Clause

The by-laws may also contain a right-of-first-refusal clause on resale of the co-op. These clauses are more common in co-ops than in condos. They hamper the free marketability of shares by requiring shareholders to offer them to the corporation before they can be sold on the open market.

Some co-op corporation also impose a "flip-tax" when a shareholder sells his or her interest.

## Interview

The by-laws of many co-ops require potential purchasers of shares to pass an interview with the co-op board or a committee of the board. (See Chapter 15.) Remember that the right to own stock carries with it the right to occupy one unit. These interviews are intensive, extensive and often embarrassing, but they do serve a purpose. Interviews offer present shareholders security and comfort in knowing that new shareholders will be scrutinized for suitability to carry their financial burden. Remember that in a co-op, the failure of one person to pay monthly fees will put more of a burden on the other owners than in the case of a condo because, in a co-op, the monthly fees include part of the mortgage payment.

However, the interviews can also be petty, humiliating and sometimes ridiculous. In addition to submitting financial statements, references, your credit rating, and your tax returns, you, your children and even your pets may be interviewed. Everyone has read stories of the New York co-ops who refused to allow famous rock stars to buy shares, because they were afraid of wild parties and undesirable guests. However, it is not only the famous who come under scrutiny and can be rejected. Anyone can be refused admission to the select co-op club, and in most areas the laws do not require the boards to tell you why you were refused.

From the standpoint of a present owner, having to get the approval of the board before you can sell can place a substantial economic burden on a shareholder who wants or needs to sell quickly.

## House Rules

Additional rules and regulations may appear in the by-laws or in a separate document called the house rules. It is urgent that you obtain copies of all regulatory documents before you decide to buy.

## Operating Budget

The operating budget will be referred to in the by-laws. An analysis of the operating budget of a co-op is exactly the same as that for a condominium, except that in a co-op, there will be a provision for repayment of the mortgage loan and property taxes. Make sure that all necessary items are covered in the operating budget. Remember the problem of low-balling (see Chapter 10).

44

## Management Contract

Management contracts for co-ops are exactly the same as those for condos. See page 38.

## Insurance

The by-laws will probably require that you get insurance on the contents of the unit you occupy, which you should do in any case. In most states, this is called homeowners insurance; occasionally it is called tenants insurance. Make sure that this insurance is in effect from the first day you begin to move your belongings into the unit, or from the first day you begin to make any alterations. Your insurance agent can obtain a "binder" for you to take immediate effect.

Of course, the co-op corporation should have adequate fire and hazard insurance on the buildings and contents, as well as several millions of dollars of public liability insurance to cover accidents on common areas.

## Stock Certificates

Ownership in a co-operative corporation is evidenced by shares of stock issued in your name. The stock certificates for a co-op look much the same as those for major corporations traded on one of the stock exchanges. Make sure that the stock certificates show the proper number of shares that you have purchased. The certificates may also show the percentage of the monthly maintenance and other expenses allocated to your shares.

You probably won't keep physical possession of the certificates. They may be held in safekeeping by the corporation or, more likely, the mortgage holder (lender) will take your certificates and those of the other owners and hold them as collateral for the mortgage loan.

## Proprietary Lease

The proprietary lease gives you the right to occupy your apartment for as long as you own shares in the co-op corporation. It is similar to a lease for renting an apartment. In this sense you can think of the co-op corporation as your landlord and you as the tenant.

While most rental leases state a specific amount of rent to be paid each month, your co-op proprietary lease will state the number of shares you own and will bind you to pay your pro rata share of the expenses on a monthly basis, as determined by the board. (Let us again stress the power of the board.) Penalties for failure to pay and procedures that the board can use will be stated. Make sure that the percentage of expenses to be borne by you as stated in the lease is the same as that stated on your stock certificate.

The lease may restate restrictions that appear in the by-laws or house rules. In addition, there may be other restrictions that appear only in the lease. These can include regulations regarding pets, guests, children, use of amenities and subletting.

## Financial Statements

The financial statements of older co-ops or the financial projections of new conversions should be analyzed in order to understand what income tax deductions you will receive for property taxes, interest and other expenses included in your monthly charges. At least once a year, accountants hired to do the corporate books will give you the exact figures you need for use in preparing your income tax.

# 15

# THE INTERVIEW

A sense of humor will be helpful to you in putting the
ritual of the co-op interview in perspective. Let us re-
mind you of Groucho Marx, who once said that he
wouldn't want to join any club that would have him as
a member. With that in mind, let's talk seriously about
the co-op interview.

Because co-operatives mean cooperation in everything, from joint payment of the mortgage to joint
ownership of the entire development, and because you
don't own anything individually in a co-op, there is
usually a strict interview requirement before the board
of directors deems you eligible to join their exclusive
club. (In a condominium, you actually own your unit,
so there is no screening of purchasers unless specifically required by the by-laws.)

The interview is a time for you and the board (or a
committee of the board) to look each other over. A potential buyer should ask questions directly and not be
intimidated.

As we said earlier, co-op boards at their worst can
be arbitrary, obnoxious, nosey and rude. Most states do
not require them to state reasons for rejecting an applicant, and you have no recourse against them in most
states unless you can prove that your rejection was
discriminatory based on race, religion, national origin
or (sometimes) sex. Discrimination is a very difficult
thing to prove.

Who can forget the Manhattan co-op that turned
down former President Richard M. Nixon? Obviously,
Mr. Nixon could afford the fees. The co-op board ap-
parently declined to admit him because they worried

that the extra security measures necessary in a building housing a former President of the United States would be a burden on the other owners and could decrease the value of their shares.

Similarly, there have been numerous stories of celebrities who have been turned down by co-op boards because of the fear of loud parties or drugs. All these decisions are much less capricious when you consider them from the point of view of an owner and neighbor.

## Dress Appropriately

Before your interview, you should try to understand the board's philosophy regarding money, procedures, and management. The board will, of course, think that it is interviewing you, and that is as it should be. You should dress appropriately. Business clothes show that you take the process seriously. Analyze what they are wearing. Are these the type of people you want to live with? Will you be compatible with them?

The interview is sort of a summit meeting—where all parties attempt to get to know and understand each other. You must not be timid about asking questions, because your hard-earned money is at stake. And you should not be offended by the personal questions asked of you. Remember that their money, security and lifestyle also are at stake—since if one co-op shareholder goes bankrupt or cannot pay, it is up to the other shareholders to make up the difference.

Expect personal questions in the interview. Remember that these people live there and are really trying to find out if you are the kind of person they want to live with them. Don't be offended by the questioning. If you want the unit, play the game and be as positive, charming and convincing of your good nature and net worth as possible. You might ask your real estate agent or any other persons you know in the complex to give you clues as to what to expect at the interview and how to behave. If the interviewers really are offensive, then you probably don't want them for neighbors in any event.

# 16

## ESCROW AND HOW TO HANDLE IT

Escrow is the holding by an impartial party of money deposited until certain conditions are met. In the case of the sale of a co-op or condominium, the escrow consists of the good faith deposit (also called the "earnest money") that the buyer makes to seal the deal.

Specifically, when you make an offer on a co-op or condo, you propose a price at which you will buy, subject to the execution by both parties of an agreement of sale. You back up your proposal with a binder deposit—usually $500 or $1,000. If your offer is accepted, a final agreement of sale is drawn up with every detail included. After the offer and acceptance and the final agreement should come a period during which the buyer has the right to have the property inspected by an inspection service or engineer, or whomever the buyer selects. The result of this inspection may allow the buyer to withdraw the offer, if the terms of the offer so provide.

Assuming all goes well, and the sale documents are signed, the buyer must then put up a good faith deposit of 10% (usually) of the sale price, by check or in cash. This money is *escrowed*—that is, held on deposit—by an escrow agent agreed upon by the buyer and seller until closing.

### Who Holds the Escrow Money?

It is always best to have your representative in charge of the escrow money, because the person in charge is the one who releases the money once all the conditions are met. From the buyer's point of view, the best escrow agent is his or her attorney. Second best is to have the money held jointly by the buyer's and the seller's attorney. If the co-op or condo is a new one, the seller's lending institution often handles the escrow. In some states, the real estate agent customarily holds the escrow. You may not have a choice, but, as we said, it's always best to have your own person control the escrow if you can.

The time between the signing of the agreement of sale and the actual settlement is usually 60 to 90 days, but it can be shorter or longer, depending on the needs of the people involved. Who earns interest on the escrowed money? Unless state or local law or custom provide otherwise, the recipient of the escrow interest is open to negotiation and should be spelled out in the sale documents. Since there is no clear standard, we know of many situations when the judgment of Solomon worked best and the escrow interest was split evenly between buyer and seller.

# 17

# CALCULATING YOUR DOWN PAYMENT

When you buy any property, one of the critical decisions you must make is how much of the purchase price you will pay in cash (the down payment) and how much you will borrow (the mortgage or co-op loan).

## Down Payments—Large and Small

There are two schools of thought regarding how large a down payment you should make.

Those who favor large down payments say that real estate is a marvelous investment and the sooner you own the property, the better. A large down payment gives you immediate equity, or financial ownership, in the property. A larger down payment may help you to qualify for a mortgage or co-op loan on better terms than you might otherwise get, possibly at a lower interest rate. And obviously, a larger down payment will result in a smaller loan and lower monthly payments.

Those who favor small down payments are urging you, in effect, to take advantage of your status as an owner to borrow more rather than less. They point out that the higher monthly payments are less of a burden than might appear, since, especially at the beginning, the payments are largely interest on the loan, and are tax-deductible.

A small down payment obviously gives you more leverage. You have bought a large asset with relatively little cash. If you want to buy a co-op or condo that is expensive relative to your available cash, you have no choice but to make a small down payment.

A small down payment lets you stay more liquid. Instead of having all your savings tied up in the co-op or condo, you can keep part of your savings working for you in investments that produce income, such as bank accounts, stocks, or mutual funds. These assets are liquid—that is, they are readily available to you should you need them for expenses or emergencies—and the extra income may offset (or even more than offset) the higher monthly payments. However, if you invest the money carelessly, you may wish that you had used it for a larger down payment instead.

The decision as to how large a down payment to make will ultimately depend on you and your individual financial needs. It is a good idea to ask the advice of your accountant before finally deciding just how much money to put down.

# 18

## FINANCING CO-OPERATIVES

There is a substantial difference between financing the purchase of a condominium and a co-operative.

Because you actually own the unit you occupy in a condo, you can get a mortgage loan to finance it. You are free to pick and choose the exact type of mortgage loan and repayment schedule that suits you best. Mortgages will be discussed in Chapter 19.

Because you don't actually own a specific unit in a co-op, but occupy a unit under a proprietary lease, you cannot get a mortgage loan to finance your purchase. So, how do you finance a co-op? You get a personal loan from your bank, credit union or other financial institution. And you use your shares of stock as the collateral (security) for the repayment of the debt.

Because banks prefer mortgage obligations, you will probably find that the interest rate on personal loans to finance a co-op purchase will be somewhat higher than the going mortgage rate. Make sure that you shop around. The rates charged by the various lending institutions differ, and there are many places to choose from. Your real estate agent or attorney should be helpful in directing you to financing.

(While you can't get a mortgage on your own co-op unit, you should be aware, as a completely separate matter, that the co-op *corporation* probably has a mortgage loan on the entire property—which you, as a shareholder, help repay as a portion of your monthly fees.)

# 19

## FINANCING CONDOMINIUMS—
## MORTGAGES

For a complete discussion of mortgages we suggest that you read the No-Nonsense Real Estate Guide, *Understanding Mortgages*.

### What Is a Mortgage?

We all use the word *mortgage* for convenience when in fact we are talking about a *mortgage loan*. The mortgage itself is not a loan, but a *pledge*. This makes sense once you understand how a mortgage actually works. When we speak about "getting a mortgage," we actually mean the *mortgage loan*. A bank or other lender lends you the money for your purchase and in return you give the lender a mortgage (pledge); you have pledged your property as security for the repayment of the loan, plus any interest that has accrued on it.

The lender then registers your pledge with the appropriate local authority in the form of a *lien*. A lien is a legal notice that if the property is sold or if you fail to repay on schedule, the lien holder (lender) has a legal means, called foreclosure, of taking possession of the property in order to be repaid the amount owed.

Once the loan plus the interest has been paid off, the lien is removed and the pledged property is yours free and clear.

### Obtaining Financing

Who will help you in your quest for financing? Surprisingly, more people than you think.

## Builder or Converter

If you want a new condo, the builder or converter will probably have arranged to have mortgage money available for qualified buyers. As with any mortgage loan, you will be asked to fill out a detailed financial disclosure statement. These forms are rather standard, and two are reproduced in Appendix A.

## Seller

If you are buying an older condo, the seller will sometimes take back a mortgage, or partially assist with the financing. This can be a favorable arrangement, but make sure that your attorney draws the documents carefully.

## Buy-down

The builder or converter of a new condo may buy-down the mortgage for the buyer. This means that the builder will pay the lender the cash equivalent of one or several points of interest so that the buyer has a lower interest rate to pay on the mortgage loan.

A buy-down can be either permanent or temporary. In a permanent buy-down, the builder pays the cash equivalent of interest points for the life of the loan. More prevalent is the temporary buy-down where the interest is reduced for a specified number of years. A common scheme is to buy-down 3% in the first year of the mortgage, 2% in the second, and 1% in the third. This is an excellent deal for the buyer, who benefits directly from the reduction in mortgage payments.

## Broker

If the seller is not interested in financing, the real estate broker will often assist you in obtaining a mortgage loan. You should know that in most areas the broker receives a fee from the mortgage company in return for bringing in customers. This should not worry you, if you follow the next piece of advice to be sure that the deal you accept is the best one available.

## Shop, Shop, Shop

There is one simple rule to follow in obtaining a mortgage loan. The rule is shop, shop, shop.

## Where to Shop

Go to as many commercial banks, savings and loans, credit unions and mortgage companies as you can before you sign on the dotted line.

In addition to the banks and other institutions mentioned above, you might also go to a mortgage consultant and/or to one of the new computerized mortgage origination networks that are just developing.

## Mortgage Consultant

A mortgage consultant processes your application for subscribing lenders. Theoretically, this allows your application to be viewed by many lenders at once. There is no fee to the buyer for their service, but you should always check around to make sure that the deal they offer you is the best available.

## Computerized Mortgage Network

A computerized mortgage network offers processing plus speed. Your application data is fed into a computer terminal and a mortgage commitment can be received in as little as 30 minutes. Once again, we caution you to comparison shop before signing.

One good source of mortgage information is the mortgage reporting services that are available in many areas. They tell you where the mortgage money is, the interest rates being offered, and the qualifications you must meet for each listed lender. They can save you considerable legwork.

The advice to comparison shop for mortgage terms is especially true at this time. It used to be that mortgages were relatively standard, with fixed rates and for a fixed period of time, usually 20 to 30 years. All that uniformity has changed.

To sum up, mortgages are no longer uniform, and very different rates and "deals" are available from different lenders. This expansion of creativity in the mortgage business has led to the development of many new types of mortgages. We will discuss several of the more popular ones; but for more extensive information on mortgages, see *Understanding Mortgages.*

## Adjustable-Rate Mortgage (ARM)

The most important change has been the development of the adjustable-rate mortgage ("ARM"). While the fixed-rate mortgage still exists, a large part of the market has now been taken by the adjustable-rate mortgage (called an adjustable mortgage loan (AML) in savings and loan associations), a radically different arrangement. With an ARM, the interest rate you pay is adjusted periodically according to fluctuations in some standard interest rate index, such as the current rate on U.S. Treasury bills. An ARM makes you gamble on the trend of interest rates. If interest rates generally go down, you may end up paying less each month. But if rates go up, you will have to pay more.

Most ARMs have maximums (called "caps") on the amount by which the interest rate can be raised at each adjustment period, or over the whole life of the mortgage, or both. The caps may also be expressed as a maximum monthly payment figure. Obviously, the lower the caps, the better for the borrower.

## Negative Amortization

One major problem with ARMs is the potential for "negative amortization." Amortization is the process of paying off the principal amount of your loan; negative amortization means that the process is going the wrong way. This problem arises when the interest rate goes up, but the monthly amount that the lender can charge the borrower doesn't cover the increase—most likely because of a payment cap.

Negative amortization takes place because your monthly payments don't cover the revised interest charges on your loan, and the amount by which the payments fall short is added to the principal of the loan. So, while you are making your payments, the amount of your debt actually *increases*. Not a good situation at all.

There are four principles to remember when dealing with ARMs:

1. The lower the maximum and minimum caps are, the better.
2. A cap on the interest rate (rather than on payments) will avoid the problem of negative amortization.
3. The less frequently the interest rate is adjusted, the better.
4. The more stable the chosen index is, and the less subject to fluctuations, the better.

## Balloon Mortgage

A balloon mortgage starts out like a fixed-rate mortgage, with payments calculated as if the loan were to be paid off in 20 or 30 years. However, in a balloon mortgage, you only make your payments for a specified time—3, 5 or 10 years—after which time the entire amount of the mortgage loan becomes due and owing.

This means that when the mortgage "balloons," you have to find refinancing somewhere, and that may come at a time when mortgage rates are unfavorable to the borrower.

## Graduated Payment Mortgage (GPM)

A GPM is a popular type of mortgage with young people who expect their incomes to rise over the next few years. A GPM can be either a fixed-rate or an adjustable-rate mortgage loan. With a GPM, the amount you pay is graduated so that you pay less at the beginning of the loan, and more as the loan progresses.

You should be careful to understand how much you will eventually have to pay, and to be reasonably sure you will be able to afford it. In addition, GPMs may have a negative amortization period at the beginning that you should be aware of.

## Growing Equity Mortgate (GEM)

With a GEM, your monthly payments increase each year by a specified amount, usually 7½%. The extra 7½% is applied directly against the principal you owe, so that your equity in the property increases at a faster rate.

## Mortgage Insurance

Many lenders of non-government backed loans require the buyer to purchase private mortgage insurance (PMI). Private mortgage insurance should not be confused with mortgage *life* insurance, discussed later in this chapter. The purpose of private mortgage insurance is to guarantee that if you default on the mortgage payments, the lender will get back the full balance of the loan.

If your downpayment is less than 10% of the cost of the condo, your lender will almost certainly require you to get mortgage insurance. Insurance will also probably be required if your downpayment is between 10% and 20%.

The largest writer of mortgage insurance is the Mortgage Guarantee Insurance Company, known as MGIC (pronounced "magic"). Mortgage insurance is also written by many other companies and is sometimes provided by the lender itself.

Mortgage insurance costs have remained rather steady over time, averaging about $5 for every $1,000 of first year coverage. Insurance companies have recently begun to petition state governments to allow them to raise rates.

## Cancelling Mortgage Insurance

Most lenders require you to carry this insurance for the life of the mortgage loan. This is an unnecessary expense for a borrower whose equity in the condo has increased and whose outstanding loan principal is small compared to the value of the property. Some mortgage lenders follow a theory that when the outstanding balance on the loan is less than 80% of the purchase price, or if the balance is less than 80% of a current acceptable appraised value, insurance can be cancelled.

How much will you save by cancelling insurance? It could be as much as $125 to $175 per year. So check the mortgage contract with your lender before signing and try to see that the insurance is required only for a limited period. It will be harder to cancel insurance in situations where the lender is also the insurer. Many lenders are self-insurers and are reluctant to cancel policies that are bringing them money.

## Mortgage Life Insurance

Mortgage *life* insurance should not be confused with the private mortgage insurance discussed above. The purpose of mortgage life insurance is to guarantee that the mortgage can be paid off if you die. You may be required to take out such insurance as part of the financing deal.

Mortgage life insurance is usually a form of *decreasing term* life insurance—the simplest and cheapest life insurance with no savings element or cash value, and with the coverage decreasing each year to match the remaining principal amount of your mortgage. Again, you may be required to carry this insurance for the life of the mortgage, and again, the lender doesn't really need this protection after the first few years.

# 20

# SETTLEMENT OR CLOSING THE DEAL

Everyone seems to approach settlement (also known as closing) with fear and trepidation. Things will go properly, however, if you follow these simple rules: do your homework and go well prepared.

## What Is Settlement

Settlement is the time when the buyer becomes the actual owner of the property. Many documents are signed and much money changes hands.

## Be Prepared

Bring extra checks with you, several pens, and a calculator to check the numbers. Bring all your documents with you and check the final papers against your preliminary drafts for any discrepancies. It is a good idea to take your attorney with you so that any problems that arise can be settled on the spot.

## Good Faith Estimate

If you are buying a condominium with a mortgage loan, you will receive, within three days of applying for the loan, a good faith estimate of settlement charges. This is according to the federal Real Estate Settlement Procedures Act (RESPA). A copy of the standard RESPA form is reproduced in Appendix B.

## The Settlement Sheet

The "settlement sheet" is a document prepared at the settlement, or closing, of a real estate purchase which details all the various charges paid to and by each party to the transaction. A sample of the HUD settlement sheet is reproduced in Appendix C.

Remember that there are different rules and customs relating to which party pays what settlement costs. You should check with your lender, attorney, and real estate agent to avoid any surprises.

There are often extra costs that might not show up on the good faith estimate. These can include taxes, title search fee, mortgage and title insurance, homeowners' insurance, prepayment of utilities, attorney's fees, and adjustments. In addition, there will probably be a mortgage loan origination fee. The lender is likely to charge between 1 and 4 points, or 1% to 4%. One percent is most common. These costs usually are paid by the buyer, but custom or agreement of the parties could allow for the seller to pay them, or for each of the parties to pay one-half. Many of these charges are expressed in terms of "points," each point representing 1% of the face value of the mortgage. So, if the mortgage loan were for $50,000, one point would cost $500.

## Conclusion

Co-operative and condominium living is easy, carefree, and exciting.

We hope you enjoy your new lifestyle and we wish you happiness.

# 21

## TIME SHARING

Time sharing is a vacation idea often sold using high pressure tactics urging you to purchase your future vacations at today's prices.

How accurate is it to say that time sharing allows you to buy inflation-proof vacations forever? Time sharing can work, but it hasn't worked as well as the advertisements suggest. First, pick your location very carefully, and make sure that you are willing to go back to the same place year after year. And remember that you have to pay for your share, and a portion of the maintenance on it, whether or not you actually use it.

### What Do You Own?

There are two basic time sharing deals: ownership and right-to-use plans. In an ownership plan, you actually buy a certain number of weeks (usually one or two) in a condominium-like situation in a vacation resort.

This means that, for example, you purchase, in fee simple, one week out of a 52-week year in a resort in Florida, or a ski chalet in Aspen. You make settlement and actually get a deed and take title to the unit. However, your title is only for one-fifty-second of the total title to the property. Legally, you either own your shares as tenants in common with the other owners (also called a "time span ownership"), or as an "interval ownership." Each gives you fee simple title, title insurance and a deed.

You have the absolute right to occupy and use your unit during your week(s) each and every year, forever.

You also have the right to sell your share—if you can find a buyer.

## Flex Time

Which week(s) you choose will affect the price charged, with the more desirable weeks commanding the most money. Some resorts sell *flex time*, a plan which gives you some flexibility by letting you choose your weeks, upon confirmed reservations, within a specific season. This is also called "floating time," or "open use." In some of the flex time plans, you are entitled to a specific type of unit, but not necessarily to one particular unit.

## Right-to-Use Plans

Right-to-use plans do not give you fee ownership. Rather you purchase the right to use the property for fixed periods each year for a given number of years, usually 12 to 40. At the end of that time, the property returns to the original owner.

Right-to-use plans are of three types: vacation licenses, vacation leases, or club memberships. The differences have to do with the type of property being purchased and the rights you acquire. Vacation licenses are the most popular form of right-to-use ownership. They exist mostly in operating hotels and they are generally not resalable. Vacation leases are resalable (if a buyer can be found, which is often doubtful). Club memberships are similar to memberships in country clubs, are not resalable, and are run through nonprofit associations.

## Tax Ramifications

Time share sellers used to stress possible tax savings. However, under the Tax Reform Act of 1986, the interest you pay on money borrowed to purchase a time share portion is not deductible for federal income tax purposes. Remember, in addition, that you are also responsible for paying a portion of the yearly maintenance costs. Maintenance costs are not fixed, and are likely to go up over the years.

## Swapping

One much publicized advantage of time sharing is the ability to swap with other time sharers around the world. Time sharing ventures exist in at least 38 countries worldwide, and about 75% of these have exchange options. Can you really swap your week in Florida for a week in Greece? Perhaps, but of course you will only get an attractive swap if you have something equally attractive to give up in exchange.

As of this writing, three companies specialize in organizing swaps. Developers pay a fee to affiliate their development with one of these exchanges. This fee depends on the nature, size and quality of the project and usually ranges from $6500 to $9000. Then, for a fee—usually about $45 to $55 per swap—an individual time share owner can try to trade the use of his or her time share for one of equal value in another resort. These companies match up willing participants through their network of member resorts:

Resorts Condominium International (RCI)
9333 North Meridian Street
P.O. Box 80229
Indianapolis, Indiana 46280
317-846-4724

Interval International
7000 S.W. 62nd Avenue
Suite 306
Miami, Florida 33142
305-666-1861

The Exchange Network
P.O. Box 8366
Rancho Santa Fe, California 92067
619-436-1142

There are two other ways to swap: through internal exchanges operated in the individual projects with affiliated companies, or through private arrangements with individual owners.

## Conclusion

We think you ought to be hesitant about time sharing. But if you are certain that you want to participate, and you want to check out the reliability of a specific deal being offered, you can contact the

National TimeSharing Council of the American
Land Development Association
1000 16th Street, N.W.
Washington, D.C. 20036

The Council has several publications, including "Resort and Urban Timesharing—A Consumer's Guide." This pamphlet costs $2.00 and is available by writing to the Council. Also available is a free bibliography and a Directory of Resorts ($7.00).

# GLOSSARY

**Abstract of Title**  A record of the title, or history of ownership, of a property.

**Adjustable Mortgage Loan (AML)**  Similar to an ARM, and offered by savings and loan associations. See Adjustable-Rate Mortgage.

**Adjustable-Rate Mortgage (ARM)**  A mortgage whose interest rate is periodically adjusted according to an agreed-upon index.

**Air Space Estate**  A term to describe what a condominium owner purchases, that is, the airspace between the exterior walls of the unit.

**Amortization**  The practice by which the principal amount of a loan is reduced through periodic repayments.

**Appraisal**  An expert evaluation of the fair market value of a property.

**Appreciation**  An increase in value of a property.

**Assessment**  The pro rata share of regular expenses paid by each condo owner as a monthly fee. Also called an Operating Assessment.

**Association**  See Condominium Association.

**Balloon Mortgage**  A type of mortgage loan where monthly payments are made until a certain date when the remaining balance becomes due and payable in full.

**Beneficial Owner**  See Equitable Owner.

**Board of Directors**  The elected governing body of a co-op.

**Board of Managers**  The elected governing body of a condominium association.

**Building Officials and Code Administrators International Code (BOCA Code)**  The building code used nationwide in most residential construction.

**Buy-down**  A procedure by which the seller of a condo, or a condo builder or converter permanently or temporarily reduces the amount of interest the buyer will have to pay by paying "points" to the mortgage lender at closing.

**Buyer-Agent**  An agent hired and paid for by the buyer of a property to find the appropriate property and negotiate for its purchase.

**By-laws**  The governing document in a co-op corporation or condominium.

**Certificate of Incorporation**  The legal document, filed with the state, that officially establishes the existence of a corporation.

**Certificate of Title**  The document which evidences ownership of a condominium unit.

**Clear Title**  See Marketable Title.

**Closing**  The time when legal title to a property passes from the seller to the buyer. (Also termed Settlement.)

**Collateral**  The security for repayment of a loan. In a mortgage loan, the property is pledged (mortgaged) as security.

**Common Area**  See Common Element.

**Common Element**  Items in a condominium which are owned by all owners as undivided interests. Examples include lobby, swimming pool, elevators, roof, etc.

**Common Estate**  See Common Element.

**Common Expenses**  Expenses incurred in the operation of a condo which are shared proportionately by all owners.

**Common Property**  See Common Element.

**Common Space**  See Common Element.

**Condominium (Condo)**  A form of joint property ownership. Title to a specific condo unit is held in fee simple, with common elements jointly owned by all condo owners together.

**Condominium Association**  The elected governing body of a condominium.

**Conventional Mortgage Loan**  Any mortgage loan that does not have government backing.

**Co-operative (Co-op)**  A form of joint property ownership where the entire development is owned by a co-operative corporation whose shareholders have the right to occupy individual units.

**Corporate Charter**  See Certificate of Incorporation.

**Declaration**  The legal document which creates a condominium, filed with the state.

**Deed**  The piece of paper filed according to law which evidences title (ownership) of a property.

**Down Payment**  Cash payable by the buyer of a property equal to the difference between the total sale price and the amount of the mortgage loan.

**Earnest Money**  The deposit given by the buyer to the seller to show serious intent to purchase.

**Easement**  The right to enter or use a portion of the land of another for a specific purpose.

**Encumbrance**  Any claim, charge, lien or liability against a property.

**Equitable Owner** The person who has signed an agreement of sale for a property but who does not as yet hold legal title to it.

**Equity or Owner's Equity** The amount by which the present value of the property exceeds the amount of the mortgage and all other debts, claims or liens against the property.

**Escrow** Money deposited and held by a neutral party until certain purchase conditions are met.

**Federal Home Loan Mortgage Corporation (Freddie Mac)** A quasi-governmental agency which purchases mortgages from the original mortgage lenders.

**Federal Housing Authority (FHA)** A part of the U.S. Department of Housing and Urban Development which offers mortgage loan insurance programs to buyers of qualifying properties.

**Federal National Mortgage Association (Fannie Mae)** A quasi-governmental agency, now publicly owned, which purchases mortgages from the original mortgage lenders.

**Fee Simple Absolute (Fee)** The best and most complete form of legal ownership, carrying the absolute right to use, sell, or bequeath property in any manner desired.

**Flip Tax** A fee paid to the co-op corporation by a shareholder who sells his/her interest in the co-op (shares and proprietary lease).

**Foreclosure** The legal remedy used by a mortgage lender to assume ownership of a property when required loan repayments are not made.

**Good Faith Deposit** See Earnest Money.

**Government National Mortgage Association (Ginnie Mae)** A quasi-governmental agency, carrying the full faith and credit of the United States government, which purchases mortgages from the original mortgage lender.

**Graduated Payment Mortgage** A type of mortgage loan where the repayments start small and gradually increase.

**Home Owners Warranty** One of the best 10-year warranties available for newly built houses.

**House Rules** Additional rules and regulations which, together with the by-laws, govern the operation of a condo or co-op.

**HUD** The U.S. Department of Housing and Urban Development.

**Joint Tenants** A form of property ownership between two

or more persons with "right of survivorship," where all can use and enjoy the whole property, and on death, the whole property is owned by the survivors.

**Leasehold Interest** The right to occupy and use a specific property under the terms and conditions stated in the lease document. Does not convey an ownership interest.

**Leverage** Using a small amount of money (capital) to obtain ownership and/or control of a large property.

**Lien** A legal notice, filed according to law, of the right of a lienholder (such as a mortgage lender) to be paid from the proceeds of the sale of property on which the lien was recorded.

**Limited Common Element** A common element in a condominium such as a terrace or parking space which, while remaining in common ownership, is assigned to one owner for exclusive use.

**Liquid Investment** An investment that can be turned into cash easily and quickly.

**Maintenance** The monthly fees paid by a co-operative shareholder.

**Marketable Title** Title to a property which renders the property free and clear and able to be transferred freely.

**Mortgage** The legal document representing a loan of money in return for the pledge of a property as collateral for the repayment of the loan with interest.

**Mortgage Commitment** The written notice from a mortgage lender that your mortgage application has been approved and that for a specified time period, the mortgage loan will be available for you to buy a specified property.

**Mortgagee** The person or company who receives the mortgage as a pledge for repayment of the loan. The mortgage lender.

**Mortgagor** The mortgage borrower who gives the mortgage as a pledge to repay.

**Multiple Listing Service (MLS)** A service where house listings of member real estate agents are made available for all agents to sell. Commissions from multiple listing sales are split between co-operating agents.

**Negative Amortization** The process of adding to the principal balance of a loan when current payments do not fully cover the required interest.

**Offering Plan** The written document, usually filed with the state, detailing the terms and conditions of a new co-operative housing corporation.

**Origination Fee** A fee, usually amounting to one to four points (1% to 4% of the amount of the mortgage loan), charged by a mortgage lender at the inception of the loan.

**Points** Charges levied by the mortgage lender and usually payable at closing. One point represents 1% of the face value of the mortgage loan.

**Par Value** An arbitrary and meaningless value assigned to stock when a corporation is formed. Often set at $1.00 per share.

**Pre-payment Penalty** A charge imposed by a mortgage lender on a borrower who wants to pay off part or all of a mortgage loan in advance of schedule.

**Principal** The face amount borrowed in a mortgage loan.

**Proprietary Lease** A lease given by a co-op corporation to a shareholder giving the right to occupy a specific unit within the co-op.

**Punch List** A list compiled by the buyer on the pre-settlement inspection, detailing all defects and problems found in a property. The list is signed by the buyer and co-signed by the builder or his or her representative.

**Real Estate Agent** An employee of a real estate broker who has passed an examination and is licensed by the state.

**Real Estate Broker** A person who has passed an advanced examination and is licensed by the state to show houses to potential buyers and to negotiate purchases and sales, and to receive fees for such services.

**Realtor** See Real Estate Broker.

**Resale Fee** See Flip Tax.

**Reserve Fund** A portion of the monthly assessment held for payment of emergencies.

**Right-of-First-Refusal** The right of a co-op board or (sometimes) a condo association to purchase a unit from the owner, prior to the owner selling his/her share or unit to the public.

**Salesperson** See Real Estate Agent.

**Settlement** See Closing.

**Special Assessment** An additional allocated amount collected from each owner or shareholder to pay for a special item or to make up a budget deficit.

**Subscription Agreement** An agreement to buy shares in a co-operative housing corporation, pursuant to an Offering Plan.

**Subscription Money** See Earnest Money.

**Survey** A legally precise description of a property including the location and size of the land and all buildings thereon.

**Tenants by the Entireties**  The legal form of ownership of property owned jointly by husband and wife.

**Tenants in Common**  A form of property ownership where two or more persons own a property and all can use or enjoy it and each tenant can will, sell or devise his or her piece as they see fit, with no right of survivorship.

**Time Share**  A form of ownership, used primarily for vacation homes, where one or several weeks of ownership or occupancy per year are purchased usually in fee simple absolute.

**Title**  Legal evidence of ownership of a property.

**Title Company**  A company which researches titles and usually also insures them against defects.

**Title Insurance**  Insurance obtained by the buyer of a house to insure against any undiscovered problems regarding title to the property.

**Title Search**  An investigation into the history of ownership of a property to check for unpaid claims, restrictions or problems.

**Transfer Fee**  See Flip Tax.

**Undivided Interest**  The type of ownership a condo owner has in common elements of the development.

**Veterans Administration (VA)**  A government agency which guarantees mortgage loans with no down payment to qualified veterans.

**Warranty**  A protection plan for the repair or replacement of defective merchandise or workmanship.

# NO-NONSENSE CONDO AND CO-OP CHECK LIST

# NO-NONSENSE CONDO AND CO-OP CHECK LIST

## GENERAL

### LOCATION

Schools _____

Churches or Synagogues _____

Shopping _____

Public Transportation _____

Bus _____

Train _____

Trolley _____

Highway _____

Accessebility _____

Entertainment _____

### FUTURE APPRECIATION

Stability of Neighborhood _____

### COMMUNITY SERVICES

Hospital _____

Location _____

Fire Department _____

Location _____

Police Department _____

Location _____

## RECREATION

CLUB MEMBERSHIP INCLUDED _____

CLUBHOUSE _____

### SWIMMING

Location _____

Noise _____

Outdoor Pool _____

Indoor Pool _____

Children's Pool _____

Lifeguard _____

### BEACH OR LAKEFRONT

Location _____

Accessibility _____

Ability to sit by lake or beach _____

### SPORTS

Tennis _____

Platform Tennis _____

Ping Pong _____

Billiards _____

Racquetball _____

Squash _____

Ambulance _____

Trash Removal _____

Sewage _____

Type of System _____

HAZARDS

Natural _____

Artificial _____

WATER QUALITY

Cost _____

TAXES

State _____

City _____

Local _____

ASSESSMENTS _____

EASEMENTS _____

NUISANCES

Noise _____

ZONING

Residential _____

Commercial _____

Basketball _____

Handball _____

Bicycle Path _____

Horseback Riding _____

Golf _____

Jogging Track _____

CHILDREN'S PLAYGROUND AND ORGANIZED
SPORTS AND ACTIVITIES

Location _____

Noise _____

# EXTERIOR COMMON ELEMENTS

SIZE OF DEVELOPMENT _____

STYLE OF DEVELOPMENT _____

DRAINAGE _____

PRIVACY _____

ROADWAY _____

Traffic _____

Private Street _____

Children's Safety _____

SIDEWALKS _____

Yes or No _____

## AUTOMOBILES

Driveway _____

Private _____

Semi-private _____

Public _____

On Street Parking _____

Off Street Parking _____

Garage _____

Reserved Space _____

One or Two Cars _____

Automated Garage Doors _____

Security _____

## CONSTRUCTION MATERIAL

Wood _____

Stone _____

Brick _____

Vinyl Siding _____

Aluminium Siding _____

## ROOF

Material _____

Age _____

Condition _____

Leaks _____

## PERSONNEL

Maintenance _____

Gardener _____

Snow Removal _____

Trash Removal _____

Security _____

Number of Guards _____

Location _____

Hours _____

Patrol _____

Front Desk _____

## ASSOCIATION

Age of Other Owners _____

Activity of Association _____

# INTERIOR COMMON ELEMENTS

## GENERAL

Intercom System _____

Burglar Alarm System _____

Fire Safety System _____

Smoke Detectors _____

Fire Alarms _____

General Safety _____

Pre-wired for Telephone and Television Cable _____

### DOWNSPOUTS AND ROOF GUTTERS
Number _____
Placement _____

### SPLASH BLOCKS
Placement _____
Sufficient to keep water from house _____

### PESTS
Termite Inspection Certificate _____
Termite Inspection Warranty _____
Termite Shield (new house) _____

### TERRACES AND PORCHES
Location _____
Privacy _____
Size _____
Open or Enclosed _____

### LAWNS AND PLANTINGS
Trees _____
Shrubbery _____
Flowers _____

# MANAGEMENT
RESIDENT MANAGER

### STAIRS
Number _____
Accessibility _____
Safety _____

### STORAGE AREAS
Location _____
Closets _____
In Other Common Area _____

### ELEVATORS
Elevator Operator _____

### LOBBY
Decor _____
Cleanliness _____

### PUBLIC HALLS
Decor _____
Condition _____
Material Used _____

### PLASTER
Free of Cracks _____
Free of Stains _____

### SOUND PROOFING

### NOISE

## PLUMBING

Works Well _____

Convenient _____

Quiet _____

Water Pressure _____

## UTILITY COSTS

Gas _____

Electric _____

Other _____

## INSULATION

(The R Factor is the measure of heating and cooling efficiency. The higher the R Factor, the more efficient).

Minimum of R-19 in walls _____

Minimum of R-30 in ceiling _____

Heat Pumps _____

## TEMPERATURE CONTROLS

Location _____

Convenience _____

Individually Controlled _____

## HEATING AND AIR CONDITIONING

Type (best type depends on area) _____

Electric _____

Gas _____

## CARPET

Color _____

Kind _____

Texture _____

Hardwood Floors _____

## LIVING ROOM

Size _____

Shape _____

Fireplace _____

Windows _____

Sunlight _____

Morning _____

Afternoon _____

Privacy _____

From Outside _____

From Rest of House _____

## DEN OR FAMILY ROOM

Size _____

Shape _____

Location _____

Fireplace _____

Windows _____

View _____

Oil _____

Hot Water _____

**WINDOWS**

Windows Insulated _____

Wood Clad _____

Vinyl Clad _____

Thermal Breaks _____

Bay Windows _____

Storm Windows _____

Screen Windows _____

# INDIVIDUAL UNIT

**LOCATION** _____

**SIZE** _____

**SITUATION OF UNIT**

Takes Advantage of Sun _____

Takes Advantage of View _____

**ACCESSIBILITY** _____

**CLOSETS**

Number _____

Location _____

Built-ins in Closets and Dressing Areas _____

Sunlight _____

Morning _____

Sunlight _____

Privacy _____

**DINING ROOM**

Location _____

Size _____

Accessibility to Kitchen _____

Windows _____

View _____

**BEDROOMS**

Number _____

Location _____

Size _____

Closets _____

**BATHROOMS**

Number _____

Size _____

Materials Used _____

Shower _____

Bathtub _____

Vanity _____

Medicine Cabinet _____

Closet _____

Storage Space _____

## MASTER BEDROOM

Size _____

Shape _____

Closets _____

Location _____

Privacy _____

Fireplace _____

Floor and Wall Covering _____

## MASTER BATHROOM

Size _____

Location _____

Materials Used _____

Bathtub _____

Whirlpool _____

Jacuzzi _____

Steam _____

Shower _____

Vanity _____

Double or Single _____

Integrated Sink Bowls _____

Medicine Cabinet _____

Accessibility _____

Warranty _____

Sink _____

Material _____

Size _____

Single or Double Bowl _____

Built-in Cutting Boards _____

Appliances _____

Oven _____

Single or Double _____

Self-cleaning _____

Gas or Electric _____

Brand _____

Age _____

Warranty _____

Microwave _____

Size _____

Brand _____

Age _____

Warranty _____

Refrigerator-Freezer _____

Size and Capacity _____

Brand _____

Age _____

Single or double door _____

Storage Space _____

Closet _____

## KITCHEN

Size _____

Eat-in or Not _____

Floors

Wood _____

Linoleum _____

Tile _____

Exhaust System _____

Work Space _____

Counter Tops _____

material _____

built-ins _____

warranty _____

Kitchen Cabinets _____

Number _____

Material _____

Frost-free _____

Ice Maker _____

Warranty _____

Dishwasher _____

Brand _____

Age _____

Warranty _____

Trash Compactor _____

Brand _____

Warranty _____

Pantry or Storage Area _____

## LAUNDRY ROOM

Work Space _____

Clothes Washer and Dryer _____

Brand _____

Size and Capacity _____

Warranty _____

## DOCUMENTATION

IN ADDITION TO FNMA'S STANDARD DOCUMENTATION REQUIREMENTS, THE FOLLOWING EXHIBITS/COMMENTS ARE BEING FORWARDED IN SUPPORT OF THIS SUBMISSION:

EXHIBITS

A. _____

B. _____

C. _____

D. _____

UNDERWRITING CONSIDERATIONS

PROPERTY _____
_____
_____
_____
_____

MORTGAGOR APPLICANT(S) _____
_____
_____
_____

DELEGATED UNDERWRITING ONLY: SPECIAL CONDITIONS/REQUIREMENTS SELLER IMPOSED FOR LOAN APPROVAL
_____
_____
_____
_____

## UPON REVIEW OF THIS SUBMISSION

FNMA REVIEWER
(SIGNATURE) _____ REVIEWER NUMBER _____ ACTION DATE ___/___/___

A COMPLETED APPLICATION WAS RECEIVED BY FNMA ON _____
(DATE)

01☐ THE SUBMISSION HAS BEEN APPROVED.

SUBJECT TO THE FOLLOWING CONDITIONS:

1☐ SELLER MUST INCLUDE WITH DELIVERY APPRAISER'S CERTIFICATION THAT PROPERTY WAS COMPLETED IN ACCORDANCE WITH PLANS AND SPECIFICATIONS AS IDENTIFIED ON APPRAISAL REPORT.

2☐ SELLER MUST INCLUDE WITH DELIVERY ITS CERTIFICATION INDICATING REPAIRS TO THE PROPERTY AS STATED IN THE APPLICATION OR APPRAISAL REPORT HAVE BEEN SATISFACTORILY COMPLETED.

3☐ SELLER MUST INCLUDE WITH DELIVERY EVIDENCE THAT SALE OF BORROWER'S PREVIOUS RESIDENCE HAS BEEN COMPLETED, RESULTING IN NET PROCEEDS OF $_____ .

4☐ OTHER: _____
_____
_____

02☐ THE SUBMISSION HAS BEEN RETURNED AT YOUR REQUEST.

☐ THE SUBMISSION HAS BEEN DECLINED FOR THE REASON(S) STATED BELOW

**CREDIT**
03☐ NO CREDIT FILE
04☐ INSUFFICIENT CREDIT REFERENCES
05☐ INSUFFICIENT CREDIT FILE
06☐ UNABLE TO VERIFY CREDIT REFERENCES
07☐ GARNISHMENT, ATTACHMENT, FORECLOSURE, REPOSSESSION OR SUIT
08☐ INSUFFICIENT INCOME FOR TOTAL OBLIGATIONS
09☐ UNACCEPTABLE PAYMENT RECORD ON PREVIOUS MORT-GAGE
10☐ LACK OF CASH RESERVES
11☐ DELINQUENT CREDIT OBLIGATIONS
12☐ BANKRUPTCY
☐ INFORMATION FROM A CONSUMER REPORTING AGENCY
ADDITIONAL COMMENTS: _____
_____
_____
_____

**EMPLOYMENT STATUS**
19☐ UNABLE TO VERIFY EMPLOYMENT
20☐ LENGTH OF EMPLOYMENT
21☐ INSUFFICIENT STABILITY OF INCOME
**INCOME**
24☐ INSUFFICIENT INCOME FOR MORTGAGE PAYMENTS
25☐ UNABLE TO VERIFY INCOME
**RESIDENCY**
28☐ SECONDARY RESIDENCE
**PROPERTY**
33☐ UNACCEPTABLE PROPERTY
34☐ INSUFFICIENT DATA-PROPERTY
35☐ UNACCEPTABLE APPRAISAL
36☐ UNACCEPTABLE LEASEHOLD ESTATE
**OTHER**
37☐ INSUFFICIENT FUNDS TO CLOSE THE LOAN
38☐ CREDIT APPLICATION INCOMPLETE
39☐ WE DO NOT GRANT CREDIT TO ANY APPLICANT ON THE TERMS AND CONDITIONS YOU REQUEST

# Appendix A—Part II
## APPLICATION TO QUALIFY FOR FHA MORTGAGE

| U.S. DEPARTMENT OF HOUSING AND URBAN DEVELOPMENT<br>HOUSING — FEDERAL HOUSING COMMISSIONER<br>**MORTGAGE CREDIT ANALYSIS WORKSHEET** | CASE NUMBER |
|---|---|

### SECTION I — LOAN DATA

| 1. NAME OF BORROWER AND CO-BORROWER | 2. AMOUNT OF MORTGAGE | 3. CASH DOWN PAYMENT ON PURCHASE PRICE |
|---|---|---|
| | $ | $ |

### SECTION II — BORROWER'S/CO-BORROWER'S PERSONAL AND FINANCIAL STATUS

| 4. BORROW-ER'S AGE | 5. OCCUPATION OF BORROWER | | 6. NO. OF YRS. AT PRESENT ADDRESS | 7. ASSETS AVAILABLE FOR CLOSING | 8. CURRENT MONTHLY RENTAL OR OTHER HOUSING EXPENSE |
|---|---|---|---|---|---|
| 9. IS CO-BORROWER EMPLOYED? | 10. CO-BORROWER'S AGE | 11. OCCUPATION OF CO-BORROWER | 12. NO. OF YEARS AT PRESENT EMPLOYMENT | 13. OTHER DEPENDENTS (a) Ages_____ (b) Number_____ | |

### SECTION III — ESTIMATED MONTHLY SHELTER EXPENSES (This Property)

| | 14. TERM OF LOAN (Months) | 16. SETTLEMENT REQUIREMENTS | |
|---|---|---|---|
| 15. (a) Principal and Interest | $ | (a) Existing Debt (Refinancing ONLY) | $ |
| (b) FHA Mortgage Insurance Premium | $ | (b) Sale Price (Realty ONLY) | $ |
| (c) Ground Rent (Leasehold ONLY) | $ | (c) Repairs and Improvements | $ |
| (d) TOTAL DEBT SERVICE (A + B + C) | $ | (d) Closing Costs | $ |
| (e) Hazard Insurance | $ | (e) TOTAL ACQUISITION COST (A + B + C + D) | $ |
| (f) Taxes, Special Assessments | $ | (f) Mortgage Amount | $ |
| (g) TOTAL MTG. PAYMENT (D + E + F) | $ | (g) Borrower(s) Required Investment (E minus F) | $ |
| (h) Maintenance and Common Expense | $ | (h) Prepayable Expenses | $ |
| (i) Heat and Utilities | $ | (i) Non-Realty and Other Items | $ |
| (j) TOTAL HSG. EXPENSE (G + H + I) | $ | (j) TOTAL REQUIREMENTS (G + H + I) | $ |
| (k) Other Recurring Charges (explain) | $ | (k) Amount paid ☐ cash ☐ other (explain) | $ |
| (l) TOTAL FIXED PAYMENT (j + K) | $ | (l) Amt. to be paid ☐ cash ☐ other (explain) | $ |
| | | (m) TOTAL ASSETS AVAILABLE FOR CLOSING | $ |

### SECTION IV — MONTHLY EFFECTIVE INCOME / SECTION V — DEBTS AND OBLIGATIONS

| | | | ITEM | ✓ | Monthly Payment | Unpaid Balance |
|---|---|---|---|---|---|---|
| 17. Borrower's Base Pay | $ | | 25. State and Local Income Taxes | | $ | $ |
| 18. Other Earnings (explain) | $ | | 26. Social Security/Retirement | | | |
| 19. Co-Borrower's Base Pay | $ | | 27. | | | |
| 20. Other Earnings (explain) | $ | | 28. | | | |
| 21. Income, Real Estate | $ | | 29. | | | |
| 22. TOTAL MONTHLY EFFECTIVE INCOME | $ | | 30. | | | |
| 23. Less Federal Tax | $ | | 31. | | | |
| 24. NET EFFECTIVE INCOME | $ | | 32. | | | |

### SECTION VI — BORROWER RATING

| 34. Borrower Rating | | 33. | TOTAL | | $ | $ |
|---|---|---|---|---|---|---|
| 35. Credit Characteristics | | 39. FINAL | | 40. Loan to Value Ratio _____ % | | 43. ☐ Ratio of Net Effective Income to: |
| 36. Adequacy of Eff. Income | | ☐ Approve Application | | | | Total Housing Expense _____ % |
| 37. Stability of Eff. Income | | ☐ Reject Application | | 41. Total Payment to Rental Value _____ % | | Total Fixed Payment _____ % |
| 38. Adequacy of Available Assets | | | | 42. Debt Service to Rental Income _____ % | | |

*(Section VII-Ratios appears vertically between columns 39 and 40)*

44. REMARKS (Use reverse, if necessary)   First Time Home Buyer? ☐ Yes ☐ No

| 45. SIGNATURE OF EXAMINER | 46. DATE |
|---|---|

RETAIN ORIGINAL IN CASE BINDER, FORWARD COPY TO MANAGEMENT INFORMATION SYSTEMS DIVISION WITH HUD-92900-8

HUD-92900-WS (5-81)

# APPENDIX B
## GOOD FAITH ESTIMATE OF SETTLEMENT COSTS

Colonial Name
_____

Branch Office Address
_____

Telephone Number

### GOOD FAITH ESTIMATE OF SETTLEMENT COSTS

APPLICANT(S) _____ DATE _____

PROPERTY ADDRESS _____

SALES PRICE _____ LOAN AMOUNT _____

NOTICE - THIS FORM DOES NOT COVER ALL ITEMS YOU WILL BE REQUIRED TO PAY IN CASH AT SETTLEMENT, FOR EXAMPLE, DEPOSIT IN ESCROW FOR REAL ESTATE TAXES AND INSURANCE. YOU MAY WISH TO INQUIRE AS TO THE AMOUNT OF OTHER SUCH ITEMS. YOU MAY BE REQUIRED TO PAY OTHER ADDITIONAL AMOUNTS AT SETTLEMENT

THIS GOOD FAITH ESTIMATE OF SETTLEMENT COSTS IS MADE PURSUANT TO THE REQUIREMENTS OF THE REAL ESTATE SETTLEMENT PROCEDURES ACT. THESE FIGURES ARE ONLY ESTIMATES AND THE ACTUAL CHARGES DUE AT SETTLEMENT MAY BE DIFFERENT.

| | L. SETTLEMENT CHARGES | | |
|---|---|---|---|
| | **800. ITEMS PAYABLE IN CONNECTION WITH THE LOAN** | | **AMOUNT** |
| 801. | Loan Origination Fee | % | $ |
| 802. | Loan Discount | % | |
| 803. | Appraisal Fee | | |
| 804. | Credit Report Fee | | |
| 805. | Lender's Inspection Fee | | |
| 806. | Mortgage Insurance Application Fee | | |
| 807. | Assumption Fee | | |
| 808. | Application Fee | | |
| 809. | VA Funding Fee | | |
| 810. | HUD Mortgage Insurance Premium | | |
| 811. | | | |
| | **900. ITEMS REQUIRED BY LENDER TO BE PAID IN ADVANCE** | | |
| 901. | Interest from to @ /day | | |
| 902. | Mortgage Insurance Premium for months to | | |
| | **1100. TITLE CHARGES** | | |
| 1101. | Settlement or closing fee | | |
| 1102. | Abstract or Title search | | |
| 1103. | Title Examination | | |
| 1104. | Title Insurance Binder | | |
| 1105. | Document Preparation | | |
| 1106. | Notary Fees | | |
| 1107. | Attorney's fees (including above items numbers; ) | | |
| 1108. | Title Insurance (including above items numbers; ) | | |
| 1109. | Lender's Coverage | | |
| 1110. | Owner's Coverage | | |
| 1111. | Endorsement(s): | | |
| 1112. | | | |
| | **1200. GOVERNMENT RECORDING AND TRANSFER CHARGES** | | |
| 1201. | Recording Fees: Deed $ Mortgage $ Release $ | | |
| 1202. | City/County Tax/Stamps Deed $ Mortgage $ | | |
| 1203. | State Tax/Stamps Deed $ Mortgage $ | | |
| 1204. | | | |
| | **1300. ADDITIONAL SETTLEMENT CHARGES** | | |
| 1301. | Survey | | |
| 1302. | Pest Inspection | | |
| 1303. | Amortization Schedule | | |
| 1304. | | | |
| 1305. | | | |

**TOTAL ESTIMATED SETTLEMENT CHARGES**      $ _____

I HEREBY ACKNOWLEDGE THAT I HAVE RECEIVED A COPY OF THIS GOOD FAITH ESTIMATE OF SETTLEMENT COSTS AND A COPY OF THE HUD GUIDE FOR HOME BUYERS "SETTLEMENT COSTS AND YOU".

_____ _____ _____ _____
APPLICANT'S SIGNATURE   DATE   APPLICANT'S SIGNATURE   DATE

IF MAILED, BY:_____
                                    DATE

(G15A)

# APPENDIX C

| A. | B. TYPE OF LOAN |
|---|---|

**B. TYPE OF LOAN**

1. ☐ FHA    2. ☐ FMHA    3. ☐ CONV. UNINS.
4. ☐ VA    5. ☐ CONV. INS.

6. FILE NUMBER    7. LOAN NUMBER

**DISCLOSURE/SETTLEMENT STATEMENT**
U.S. DEPARTMENT OF HOUSING AND URBAN DEVELOPMENT - APRIL '75

8. MORTG. INS. CASE NO.

If the Truth-in-Lending Act applies to this transaction, a Truth-in-Lending statement is attached as page 3 of this form.

C. NOTE: This form is furnished to you prior to settlement to give you information about your settlement costs, and again after settlement to show the actual costs you have paid. The present copy of the form is:

STATEMENT OF ACTUAL COSTS. Amounts paid to and by the settlement agent are shown. Items marked "(p.o.c.)" were paid outside the closing; they are shown here for informational purposes and are not included in totals.

| D. NAME OF BORROWER | E. SELLER | F. LENDER |
|---|---|---|

| G. PROPERTY LOCATION | H. SETTLEMENT AGENT | I. DATES | |
|---|---|---|---|
| | | LOAN COMMITMENT | ADVANCE DISCLOSURE |
| | PLACE OF SETTLEMENT | SETTLEMENT | DATE OF PRORATIONS IF DIFFERENT FROM SETTLEMENT |

| J. SUMMARY OF BORROWER'S TRANSACTION | K. SUMMARY OF SELLER'S TRANSACTION |
|---|---|
| 100. GROSS AMOUNT DUE FROM BORROWER: | 400. GROSS AMOUNT DUE TO SELLER: |
| | 401. Contract sales price |
| 101. Contract sales price | 402. Personal property |
| 102. Personal property | 403. |
| 103. Settlement charges to borrower (from line 1400, Section L) | 404. |
| 104. | Adjustments for items paid by seller in advance: |
| 105. | 405. City/town taxes              to |
| | 406. |
| Adjustments for items paid by seller in advance: | 407. |
| 106. City/town taxes              to | 408. Water              to |
| 107. | 409. Sewer              to |
| 108. | 410.              to |
| 109. Water              to | 411.              to |
| 110. Sewer              to | 420. GROSS AMOUNT DUE TO SELLER |
| 111.              to | 500. REDUCTIONS IN AMOUNT DUE TO SELLER: |
| 112.              to | 501. Deposit or earnest money received |
| 120. GROSS AMOUNT DUE FROM BORROWER: | 502. Payoff of first mortgage loan |
| 200. AMOUNTS PAID BY OR IN BEHALF OF BORROWER: | 503. Payoff of second mortgage loan |
| 201. Deposit or earnest money | |
| 202. Principal amount of new loan(s) | 504. Settlement charges to seller (from line 1400, Section L) |
| 203. Existing loan(s) taken subject to | |
| 204. | 505. Existing loan(s) taken subject to |
| 205. | 506. |
| Credits to borrower for items unpaid by seller: | 507. |
| 206. City/town taxes              to | 508. |
| 207. | 509. |
| 208. | |
| 209. Water              to | |
| 210. Sewer              to | Credits to buyer for items unpaid by seller: |
| 211.              to | 510. City/town taxes              to |
| 212.              to | 511.              to |
| 220. TOTAL AMOUNTS PAID BY OR IN BEHALF OF BORROWER: | 512.              to |
| | 513. Water              to |
| 300. CASH AT SETTLEMENT REQUIRED FROM OR PAYABLE TO BORROWER: | 514. Sewer              to |
| | 515.              to |
| 301. Gross amount due from borrower (from line 120) | 520. TOTAL REDUCTIONS IN AMOUNT DUE TO SELLER: |
| | 600. CASH TO SELLER FROM SETTLEMENT: |
| 302. Less amounts paid by or in behalf of borrower (from line 220) | 601. Gross amount due to seller (from line 420) |
| 303. CASH ( ☐ REQUIRED FROM) OR | 602. Less total reductions in amount due to seller (from line 520) |
| ( ☐ PAYABLE TO) BORROWER: | 603. CASH TO SELLER FROM SETTLEMENT |

| L. SETTLEMENT CHARGES | PAID FROM BORROWER'S FUNDS | PAID FROM SELLER'S FUNDS |
|---|---|---|
| **700. SALES BROKER'S COMMISSION** based on price $      @    % | | |
| 701. Total commission paid by seller | | |
| Division of commission as follows: | | |
| 702. $      to | | |
| 703. $      to | | |
| 704. | | |
| **800. ITEMS PAYABLE IN CONNECTION WITH LOAN** | | |
| 801. Loan Origination fee    % | | |
| 802. Loan Discount    % | | |
| 803. Appraisal Fee to | | |
| 804. Credit Report to | | |
| 805. Lender's inspection fee | | |
| 806. Mortgage Insurance application fee to | | |
| 807. Assumption fee | | |
| 808. | | |
| 809. | | |
| 810. | | |
| 811. | | |
| **900. ITEMS REQUIRED BY LENDER TO BE PAID IN ADVANCE.** | | |
| 901. Interest from    to    @ $    /day | | |
| 902. Mortgage insurance premium for    mo. to | | |
| 903. Hazard insurance premium for    yrs. to | | |
| 904. | | |
| 905. | | |
| **1000. RESERVES DEPOSITED WITH LENDER FOR:** | | |
| 1001. Hazard insurance    mo. @ $    /mo. | | |
| 1002. Mortgage insurance    mo. @ $    /mo. | | |
| 1003. City property taxes    mo. @ $    /mo. | | |
| 1004. County property taxes    mo. @ $    /mo. | | |
| 1005. Annual assessments    mo. @ $    /mo. | | |
| 1006.    mo. @ $    /mo. | | |
| 1007. | | |
| 1008. | | |
| **1100. TITLE CHARGES:** | | |
| 1101. Settlement or closing fee to | | |
| 1102. Abstract or title search to | | |
| 1103. Title examination to | | |
| 1104. Title insurance binder to | | |
| 1105. Document preparation to | | |
| 1106. Notary fees to | | |
| 1107. Attorney's Fees to | | |
| (includes above items No.: | | |
| 1108. Title insurance to | | |
| (includes above items No.: | | |
| 1109. Lender's coverage    $ | | |
| 1110. Owner's coverage    $ | | |
| 1111. | | |
| 1112. | | |
| 1113. | | |
| **1200. GOVERNMENT RECORDING AND TRANSFER CHARGES** | | |
| 1201. Recording fees: Deed $    ; Mortgage $    Release $ | | |
| 1202. | | |
| 1203. State tax/stamps: Deed $    to: | | |
| 1204. | | |
| **1300. ADDITIONAL SETTLEMENT CHARGES** | | |
| 1301. Survey to | | |
| 1302. Pest inspection to | | |
| 1303. | | |
| 1304. | | |
| 1305. | | |
| **1400. TOTAL SETTLEMENT CHARGES** (entered on lines 103 and 503, Sections J and K) | | |

*NOTE: Under certain circumstances the borrower and seller may be permitted to waive the 12-day period which must normally occur between advance disclosure and settlement. In the event such a waiver is made, copies of the statements of waiver, executed as provided in the regulations of the Department of Housing and Urban Development, shall be attached to and made a part of this form when the form is used as a settlement statement.*

Seller

Seller      Purchaser

Address      Address      Purchaser

# ABOUT THE AUTHORS

PHYLLIS C. KAUFMAN, the originator of the *No-Nonsense Guides*, is a Philadelphia attorney and theatrical producer. A graduate of Brandeis University, she was an editor of the law review at Temple University School of Law. She is listed in *Who's Who in American Law, Who's Who of American Women*, and *Foremost Women of the Twentieth Century*.

ARNOLD CORRIGAN, noted financial expert, is the author of *How Your IRA Can Make You a Millionaire* and a frequent guest on financial talk shows. A senior officer of a large New York investment advisory firm, he holds Bachelor's and Master's Degrees in economics from Harvard and has written for Barron's and other financial publications.